Recruitment, Retention, and Employee Relations

Recruitment, Retention, and Employee Relations

FIELD-TESTED STRATEGIES for the '90s

D. KEITH DENTON

QUORUM BOOKS

WESTPORT, CONNECTICUT • LONDON

Library of Congress Cataloging-in-Publication Data

Denton, D. Keith.
    Recruitment, retention, and employee relations : field-tested
strategies for the '90s / D. Keith Denton.
      p. cm.
    Includes bibliographical references and index.
    ISBN 0–89930–661–6 (alk. paper)
    1. Personnel management.   I. Title.
HF5549.D4365   1992
658.3—dc20   92–162

British Library Cataloguing in Publication Data is available.

Library of Congress Catalog Card Number: 92–162
ISBN: 0–89930–661–6

First published in 1992

Quorum Books, 88 Post Road West, Westport, CT, 06881
An imprint of Greenwood Publishing Group, Inc.

Printed in the United States of America

The paper used in this book complies with the
Permanent Paper Standard issued by the National
Information Standards Organization (Z39.48–1984).

10 9 8 7 6 5 4 3 2 1

Thanks to my family and friends,
especially Joanne Pijut and Anita Looney.

Contents

Preface

This book is designed to help you use human resources as a competitive weapon. It is packed with powerful and proven strategic tools for improving performance through recruitment, retention, and improved employee relations. Within these pages are the stories of highly successful U.S. and foreign companies and a wide array of techniques, including:

- Merck's Interview Skills Workshop
- HP's Behavioral Interviewing
- SRC's decentralized hiring
- Marriott's recruitment programs
- Federal Express's Guaranteed Fair Treatment Procedure
- G.E.'s Work Out program
- Motorola's Six Sigma program
- Merck's flextime program
- American Express's Tracking Reports and Performance Review System
- Metropolitan Life Insurance Company's Team-Building Process
- Cypress's goal-setting process
- SRC's use of budgets and income statements
- Merck's Face-to-Face communication program
- HP's, Federal Express's, and American Express's recognition activities
- PepsiCo's SharePower

Additionally a wide range of techniques are examined which should help you:

- manage diversity within the workplace
- simplify work
- reduce turnover
- build employee self-esteem
- set up multiskilled teams
- improve employee communication
- better understand and innovate recognition and compensation systems

Recruitment, Retention, and Employee Relations

1

Crises, Cures, and Success Stories

PepsiCo's chief executive, Wayne Calloway, in discussing all the changes the corporation had made in recent years, said, "Nothing focuses the mind better than the constant sight of a competitor who wants to wipe you off the maps" (Sellers 1991, 63). As a result of this attitude, PepsiCo not only reacts to its competitor's every move but also frequently revamps operations, marketing, and manufacturing, even when things look OK. As Calloway says, "In today's economy, if it ain't broke, you might as well break it yourself because it soon will be" (63).

Acceptance of change has led to much of PepsiCo's success. Today the need for change is self-evident. In many cases, both domestic and foreign competitors are acting as the agents of change. Consider the fact that a decade ago 94 percent of the computers bought in the United States were made in the United States; in 1990 that figure was down to 66 percent. Beyond those figures is the fact that computers today are often hollowed out and full of Asian parts.

Even some made-in-America products are not what they seem. Some of these products are assembled by $6-a-day *maquiladora* (American owned and operated company inside Mexico) employees just inside Mexico. Even 300,000 American flags were imported from Taiwan and other foreign countries (Faltermayer 1990).

Foreign competition is tough and getting tougher. According to *Fortune* magazine, America has lost ground to foreign imports in both high technology and other industries. Everyone already knows about the trouble U.S. automakers are having, but many others are being challenged.

U.S. high technology's market share of telephone equipment dropped from 95 percent in 1979 to 81 percent in 1989. In this same ten-year span, U.S. semiconductor market share dropped from 90 percent to 67 percent, and the U.S. share of machine tools went from 77 percent to 54 percent. We also lost market share in other high-tech markets in the chemical, aerospace, and drug businesses. Among other markets, we have lost market share in apparel (from 86 percent to 74 percent), industrial machinery (from 95 percent to 83 percent), color T.V. sets (92 percent to 74 percent), and household appliances (92% to 81%). In all, in the 1980s we imported some $920 billion more in merchandise than we exported (Stewart 1991).

We are living well above our means. One way to prop up our standard of living is to take money from abroad, and did we ever! By 1990, the total stock of foreign investments in U.S. securities, bonds, factories, and real estate jumped to $986 million, versus $235 million in 1980 (Stewart 1991).

Perhaps the most shocking fact is that more and more of America's income will go to people living abroad. In 1991, the federal government alone paid foreigners $38 billion in interest in its debt. That amount is equal to nearly 20 percent of what U.S. manufacturers will invest in capital goods and facilities (Stewart 1991).

GOOD NEWS

In the face of all this, what could possibly be good news? The answer: U.S. business faces a serious crisis, but Americans love a crisis. In the face of these crises many U.S. companies have responded in dynamic fashion. Everyone is talking about our losing our manufacturing base, but by the end of the 1980s manufacturing accounted for 23 percent of the gross national product—a slightly higher figure than in 1980. The main reason was that productivity among manufacturers rose 3.9 percent a year in the 1980s. That is good news.

Other good news includes the fact that foreign-owned firms (not just Japanese) employ only about 4 percent of the U.S. labor force. In 1989, the United States regained its position as the world's largest exporting nation; its exports totaled a record $398 billion in 1990. Likewise, while it is true that Japanese productivity is increasing faster than U.S. productivity, overall U.S. productivity is about half again as high as Japan's (Green 1990). U.S. balance of trade deficit dropped by $157 billion in 1987 to about $80 billion in 1991.

THINK GLOBAL

The message in all of this is that, yes, we face a crisis, but it is one we are capable of handling if we respond to the challenge. Some companies still have not seen the opportunity. Robert Mosbacher, along with many others, says that only one-third of U.S. companies that could export currently do (Stewart 1991). Unfortunately, many think they cannot compete internationally, but they are wrong. Chairman and chief executive officer (CEO) Rollie Boreham, of middle-sized Baldor Electric in Fort Smith, Arkansas, sells electric motors in over 40 countries. He says what many small exporters say: "It's a myth that exports are for the big guys only. You cannot afford not to export" (Kraar 1991, 45). He says that selling abroad lets you see what is going on over there and that it is the only way of keeping foreign rivals from surprising you in your U.S. market.

We must compete globally if we are to preserve our future. For those who choose to ignore both the challenge and the opportunity, there will be more bad news than good news. More dramatically, A. T. Kearney says, "If these companies are not annealed by the fire of global competition, they will burn in it" (Stewart 1991, 22).

No business is safe from increased domestic and foreign competition. There is even increasing foreign competition in service. Already we have international banking, telecommunications, and software. New York Life Company even sends some of its forms to Ireland for processing (Stewart 1991).

1,000 SINGLES

So how do we compete? The answer is better and more consistent management, not management that is simply looking for the big play. Dan Kaplan, president of Hertz Equipment Rental Corporation, which is an equipment rental firm, says the best way to become competitive is to "hit 1,000 singles. You almost never hit a home run to turn something around overnight, but you keep cracking away with small improvements—like the Japanese do" (Kraar 1991, 45). Kaplan improves productivity by focusing on the little things. He hates bureaucracy and paperwork and makes a point of communicating and keeping in touch. He wants his people to think and act like entrepreneurs. Kaplan's way of hitting singles may not be your or my way, but the important point is to keep coming up to bat, keep focusing on incremental improvements.

There are many powerful tools available to help management make these incremental improvements. There is a wide range of computer applications, Material Requirement Planning (MRP), Just-in-Time (JIT), Total Quality Management (TQM), and Statistical Process Control (SPC). The key to competitiveness is not the tool, but rather who holds the tool. Our competitiveness rests in the hands of all of our employees.

Robert Reich, a Harvard political economist, says that creating wealth in an increasingly global economy depends on what our people can do and that it is their skills, education, and capacity that add value (Kraar 1991). Rollie Boreman, CEO of Baldor Electric, would agree. He eliminated quality problems on the night shift by taking the advice of his workers who wanted to get off before midnight and start one and one-half hours earlier. The day workers also liked the change (Kraar 1991). Granted, moving a shift up by one and one-half hours is not always going to improve quality, but in Baldor Electric's case it did. Having faith in the advice of workers almost always pays off.

The trouble is that not enough managers have faith in the capacity of the workers. It is a lesson we should have learned from the Japanese. There are 1,400 Japanese factories in the United States. Their success has taught us of the power of cooperation between blue- and white-collar employees. What it should also teach us is that, under the right conditions, American workers can be a powerful competitive weapon. Many U.S. firms may not recognize it, but the 1,400 Japanese plants do.

The Swedish-Swiss ABB's top executive, Gerhardt Schulmeyer, knows the potential of U.S. workers. He was born in Germany and worked for Sony and Motorola before becoming head of ABB, which is a $6-billion company. He stresses that each country's workers have strengths but that "Americans beat the others (Japanese, Germans) for flexibility" (Stewart 1991, 22).

Human resource people above anyone else probably recognize that a company's people are the most important resource. Most probably recognize that if you want to be customer-focused and improve quality, it cannot be done overnight. It takes the patience of the 1,000 singles to which Kaplan referred. Incremental improvements are at the heart of Japanese ability to produce better products, even when those products were often invented in the United States. Incremental improvements do not come from JIT, MRP, SPC or even high tech; they come from people just doing their job a little better.

SUCCESS STORIES

Until we are able to recruit the best people, retain them, and improve relations, we will always run the risk of losing market share. There will be missed opportunities for those incremental improvements that are in everyone.

Today's companies must be quick, flexible, and customer-focused. Recognizing this need, some of America's best-run companies are trying to find improved ways of finding and attracting the best. Once they are acquired, the companies are looking at new ways of trying to keep them productive and motivated. Not only from a human resource viewpoint, but from the viewpoint of management in general, our greatest challenge remains to engage our current work force fully. The reason is simple:

75 percent of those people who will be working in the year 2000 are already on the job.

For us to engage our current workplace, some things must change. Tom Peters relates a story of a British pub that introduced a great customer service idea called the "100 Club." For an employee to be a member, he or she had to be able to recall 100 patrons' names and drinking habits. There was one top executive in the firm who said it was a good idea but they would be lucky to have one or two of their 20,000 employees who could accomplish the task. A few months later more than 5,000 knew more than 600 names and drinking habits, and one man could even recall 2,000 names and habits (Peters 1990).

Does this story mean we should demand more from our workers? Hardly! But it does mean we need to understand better what our people are capable of and what they need from us. They do not need punishing hours or lousy direction from the top. They do not need managers who go from one crisis to the next and whose "hot button" changes with each quarter. That situation soon produces burnout, disillusionment, and exhaustion.

What employees do need is work that gives them a sense of self-esteem. They need a chance to express their creativity and autonomy. Often what they get is something different. Wayne Calloway, CEO of PepsiCo, tells of the need to encourage innovation and flexibility by relating a story about the chief of the Federal Bureau of Investigation (FBI), J. Edgar Hoover. Calloway says the FBI chief insisted on signing off on every decision, even going so far as to specify how many inches wide that margins should be on agency memos. Says he: "One day Hoover received one memo whose margins were too small. In big red letters he scrawled an angry warning across the top: 'Watch the borders.' The next morning his frightened assistants transferred 200 FBI agents to Canada and Mexico."

Competitive pressures are forcing managers to adopt new, more flexible strategies and structures. When such changes are done right, great things can happen. Lisa Carpenter works long hours on the production floor and wears an unflattering surgical hairnet and ugly rubber boots. She makes about $20,000 a year and never gets off two days in a row. Know what? She loves her job! (Clurman 1990). How is it possible?

Every day she chooses what production task she will do. Every day "she runs the risk of getting a free back rub or having a hilarious run-in with the company's JOY GANG" (Clurman 1990, 4). Every day 7.5 percent of her company profits go to a worthy social cause, like the environment, that she helps choose. She also has free health club membership, profit sharing, college tuition, and day care. She says it's what a job should be—it's not making money; it's doing good things.

To do good things, we must understand that employees are different today than they used to be. It will be impossible to do a good job recruiting, retaining, and improving relations with employees if we do not understand these changes.

In 1990, the work force was composed of 47 percent white males, and by the year 2000 it will still be composed of 45 percent white males (Perry 1991). No change, right? Wrong. Greater diversity of the work force is sure to happen. Over the next 13 years only 15 percent of the new entrants will be white males. New workers will be predominantly women (about 60 percent of new entrants), blacks, and immigrants (Bunke 1990).

Such changes will require greater concentration on managing a more diversified work force. There will be an even greater need to find and appeal to good minority recruits. In this book we will look at some very successful companies' recruiting programs, including those of Merck and Co. and Hewlett-Packard (HP). In the next chapter we will examine how Merck, a highly successful and respected pharmaceutical company, is able to use its interviewing skills workshop to great advantage. As well as other approaches, we will also look at HP's Behavioral Interviewing System, which helps it find better employees.

RECRUITING

The important point competition teaches us is to be an aggressive recruiter; use every avenue available to find good employees. Consider how Sears handled a problem of recruitment. It was faced with a shortage of qualified repair people. Its recruitment efforts included establishing a curriculum in a Chicago vocational high school that will give juniors and seniors the training they need to go to work right after high school as beginner Sears technicians. The program includes three hours a day of vocational training in basic electronics and appliance electricity and, for some, 20 hours a week of on-the-job training at Sears Service Center. Students get paid $5.15 an hour (Perry 1991).

For seven years in Portland, Oregon, Marshall and Grant high schools have been part of a successful apprenticeship program. Approximately 70 students per year supplement academic and vocational courses with on-the-job training for 20 local employers like IBM, Providence Medical Center, and so on. High school juniors and seniors from poverty-level families must have at least a 2.0 grade point average to work up to 20 hours a week at entry-level jobs, such as receptionists or data entry clerks, and are paid entry-level wages. As a result of Portland's efforts, 500 students have completed the program, 90 percent of whom have gone on to college or work or entered the military. Companies also benefited from the arrangement. One employer, First Interstate, now employs 15 graduates full-time.

Those looking for entry-level employees cannot be too aggressive. A good place for aggressive recruiters is high school. The reason is that 75 percent of high school students do not plan to attend a four-year college (Perry 1991). Some of these aggressive recruiting tools reviewed in a later chapter include use of Adopt-A-School Program, FHA (Future Homemakers of America), JA (Junior Achievement), and career days. We will also look at how Marriott, a successful recruiter, uses other, often overlooked areas as a source of entry-level applicants.

While the majority of those you recruit will probably be entry-level employees who do not have a college degree, a substantial portion of them will have a college education. These employees will form the core of your entry-level managers. They will be our future business leaders.

Chapter 4 is the strongest advocate section in the book, for a good reason. Too many human resource people treat hiring college graduates as an automatic process. This chapter reveals the current state of college education and asks you, "Are you getting your money's worth?" This chapter makes several recommendations, including establishing certified supplier education much as you would certify any supplier.

RETENTION

If it is important to recruit good people, it is imperative to retain them. The reason is cost. Aetna, for instance, estimates its annual turnover expense at more than $100 million (Perry 1991). It is money that is mostly needed to bring employees up to speed.

One of the most effective ways of both retaining and recruiting employees is to be the employer of choice. To be one of the employers of choice, you must understand your employees' needs. One of Marriott's food divisions realized that Spanish would be the primary language for a majority of its employees, so the manager of the division recommended that all first-line supervisors become fluent in Spanish.

Being the employer of choice helps a business keep employees. You can also attract and keep employees by offering them career opportunities, job variety, responsibility, and training and by giving them a sense of ownership. In succeeding pages, we will look at those techniques used by some of America's well-run companies, including Corning, Motorola, and Federal Express, for attracting and keeping employees.

Federal Express, with a turnover rate of about 1 percent, is one of these companies that have found effective ways of keeping their employees. One of the reasons it is successful is that employees have career opportunities. Federal Express has a policy of strictly promoting from within. It also recognizes the efforts of its people through awards, open communication, and other incentives. One of its most famous, and certainly most powerful, means of keeping people is through its Guaranteed Fair Treatment Procedure (GFTOP). It is, as we shall see, a very effective grievance-handling procedure. This process, along with its Survey/Feedback/Action procedure, helps keep morale high and tenure long.

While being able to retain employees is essential, there is one particular group of employees who are critical to an organization's long-term success. These are the "hard chargers," who are highly motivated and are the heart and soul of dynamic organizations. Lately there has been a problem brewing. The organizational pyramid is flattening; there are delayering, downsizing, and often disillusionment and a lack of motivation by these hard chargers.

How do you keep highly aggressive people motivated when there are fewer rungs on the organizational ladder? In the following pages we will look at how G.E. is tackling this problem. PepsiCo and others are able to keep the interest of their high achievers by accepting "zigzagging" as a viable career path. Compaq uses its culture and focus on consensus decision making to attract and keep employees' interest. DuPont does it by giving workers more autonomy and simplifying work.

Simplify

This need to simplify and rethink how and why work is done is at the heart of our ability to keep employees and keep them motivated. While some companies have completely restructured themselves, from a more practical viewpoint, each of us can make work less work and more enjoyable by applying some simple rules for eliminating irrelevant work, reports, rules, and so forth. All it takes is the right approach and a specific problem-solving technique, which is described in Chapter 7. Along the way we will look at effective strategies used by G.E., Maids International, and Motorola.

Part of being able to keep people is the ability to understand what they want, and one of the things they want is greater flexibility. Flextime is more than simply allowing employees to change arrival and departure times. It can involve job sharing as well as other techniques. We will look not only at the scope of flextime, but also at the pros and cons of such an approach and, most importantly, how to do it, using Merck's flextime program as a model.

RELATIONS

Although this material is divided into recruitment, retention, and employee relations sections, it is hard to separate them this way. Each of these areas directly affects the other.

To retain people, we need to improve relations with employees, and therefore we need to understand what today's employees need and want. As noted earlier, employees want flexibility. Arlene Johnson, for the Conference Board, says that flexible companies will capture people and inflexible companies will lose them. Companies will have to be flexible about the types of people they recruit, and they will have to be flexible about giving them what they want.

What Employees Want

In 1990, a survey of Employee Attitudes Toward Their Jobs and Quality Improvement Program was conducted for the American Society for Quality Control (ASQC) by the Gallup Organization. It asked a key question, "How can companies improve job performance?" It found that employees do want to be involved in a variety of ways.

Thirty-three percent of those surveyed felt the most important thing their company could do to increase job performance was to let them do more to put their ideas into action. A sizable 27 percent said paying them more was the most important way of increasing performance. Another nineteen percent felt that giving them more recognition was the most important way of increasing performance, and 17 percent said the most important way was to listen to their ideas for improvements (Voss 1991).

Obviously most employees feel they have ideas that could improve performance, and just as obviously, it appears they feel most companies do not appreciate them. This last section of the book looks at a wide range of techniques for improving performance through employee relations.

First we will look in some detail at how American Express uses its culture to recruit, retain, and improve employee relations. Other effective strategies include an effective management infrastructure including use of tracking reports to monitor progress, and the creation of linkages between individual effort and the bottom line. Most importantly, though, the company is able to improve relations by recognizing what is important to employees. As one American Express executive said, the only thing (in terms of performance) that matters is an employee's self-esteem. We will look at how American Express enhances employee self-esteem through its systematic use of awards and performance reviews.

The book also provides examples of how two world-class organizations enhance employee relations and performance. One of these is America's Ford Motor Company. This company turned around its business, in large part through its employee involvement efforts. This was no small task for Ford, which was a highly unionized, highly autocratic organization. Its approach toward joint partnership shows that any business can improve performance with greater employee involvement and training.

Another highly successful company that has been able to achieve a great deal of success in the international market is Fujitsu. In the United States, Fujitsu is not as well known as Ford, but it is one of Japan's most successful corporations. Later we will examine how it built its competitive culture and how its decentralized approach works. Fujitsu's story is a lesson well worth learning. In particular, its "cross-cultural" teams and "unique teams" are potent competitive tools.

CONCLUDING THOUGHTS

Techniques used by Fujitsu to enhance human relations and performance are only a few of those that are reviewed. Other examples include multiskilled teams and how to use them. AT&T's Product Development Teams, Work Design Teams, and Hoechst Celanese Corporation's cutting edge, "self-managed, self-regulated" teams are reviewed. Details of how to operate teams are explained by using Metropolitan Life Insurance Company's successful team-building model.

Everyone says it, but few do it. The "it" is communication. Rather than talking about it, it is better to show how to do it. There are many ways to enhance the power of communication. Cypress's process of goal setting and collecting detailed operational information has proven effective. In some cases, computers, like those used by Frito-Lay, have helped. Springfield Remanufacturing Corporation's (SRC) use of budgets and income statements to improve communication and performance has caught the eye of Tom Peters. They have been so successful at it that they were featured in *INC* magazine.

Studies have shown that employees do not believe management listens to them. One company that appears to listen is Merck and Co. We will examine the details of Merck's effective Face-to-Face communication program.

As the study by ASQC showed, workers need to know management is listening. They need recognition and assurance that their efforts are respected. Among other approaches, we will look at Hewlett-Packard's approach to recognition, including its famous Management-by-Wandering-Around. We will also look at Federal Express's recognition program.

Compensation has become a big issue, with the well-publicized abuses of the Savings and Loans and excessive CEO compensation. We will examine effective compensation systems, including the innovative dual-track system used by Texas Instruments and other Pay-at-Risk and Pay-for-Knowledge programs.

Finally, the book concludes with perhaps the most exciting of human resource challenges: to create a real sense of entrepreneurial spirit within organizations. We will look at three of the more exciting examples of how an entrepreneurial spirit is being created: PepsiCo's "SharePower," Hyatt's experience in setting up "spin-off" companies, and SRC's process of helping employees actually start their own business.

REFERENCES

Bunke, Harvey C. " Pax Americana." *Business Horizons*, January-February 1990, 4.

Clurman, Carol. "More Than Just a Paycheck." *USA Weekend*, January 19–21, 1990, 4.

Faltermayer, Edmund. "Is 'Made in U.S.A.' Fading Away?" *Fortune*, September 24, 1990, 62–64.

Green, Dick, "The Real Facts About 'BASHING,' Justification, and CIM or cIM." *Industrial Engineering* 22, no. 6 (1990): 4.

Kraar, Louis. "25 Who Help the U.S. Win." *Fortune* (Special Issue), 1991, 39–45.

Perry, Nancy J. "The Workers of the Future." *Fortune* (Special Issue), 1991, 68–82.

Peters, Tom. "Competitiveness Requires Trust, Appreciation of Workers." *Springfield News Leader*, August 27, 1990, D–1.

Sellers, Patricia. "Pepsi Keeps on Going After No. 1." *Fortune*, March 11, 1991, 63.

Stewart, Thomas A. "The New American Century Where We Stand." *Fortune* (Special Issue), 1991, 14–22.

Ulrich, Dave, and Dale Lake. "Organizational Capability: Creating Competitive Advantage." *Academy of Management Executive* 5, no. 1 (February 1991): 80.

Voss, Charles E. "Applied Techniques for Higher Employee Involvement." *1991 Manufacturing Principles and Practices Seminar*. Orlando, FL, April 22–24, 1991, 177.

2

Finding and Keeping Employees

Recruiting today is taken a lot more seriously and given a lot more thought than it used to be. Motorola's case is fairly typical. It used to chart the productivity of its communication-sector employee recruiting department by the amount of money recruiters spent hiring individuals. Its goal was simple—spend as little as possible. In fact, its recruiting department's productivity did go up, but without much thought about quality. Bill Smith, Motorola quality manager and vice president, said, "If you hired an idiot for 39 cents, you would meet your goal" (Henkoff 1991, 76).

To improve quality and effectiveness, the company realized that something would have to change. Now the recruiting department measures how well its recruits subsequently do at Motorola. They want to know, "Did they turn out well, or did they need remedial help?"

Increasingly, recruiting is an essential tool; our competitors recognize that it is a competitive weapon. To land a production job at Toyota, for instance, takes at least 18 hours (Kraar 1989). Once prospective employees complete a general knowledge exam and they are tested in their attitude toward work, the company then takes the top 30 percent and scrutinizes them the way American companies do their managers. These promising candidates go in groups of 12 to interpersonal skills assessment centers run by Kentucky State University for a session on problem solving. Prospects are then given a hypothetical problem and told, for example, "that a lawn mower manufacturer has production problems. The winners ask the right questions and work together to find solutions" (Kraar 1989, 104). Candidates also go through a manufacturing exercise and are asked to improve on the method they were taught. Less than 10 percent of applicants survive the final probing interviews.

Most American firms do not go through such an extensive recruiting process as Toyota, but they are getting more serious about it. It may be just in time. It is estimated that since most of the baby boomers now hold jobs, the work force will slow way down from 2.4 percent in the 1980s to 1.2 percent in the 1990s. The Bureau of Labor Statistics estimates the number of jobs will grow faster than the labor force (Main 1988). Companies will have to appeal to different groups, notably women and minorities, who will make up two-thirds of the new work force. Finding and keeping quality employees are the battle cry of the 1990s.

Frank Doyle, the senior vice president of corporate relations at General Electric, says, "For U.S. corporations, tomorrow's competitive battle will be won or lost on the strength of their ability to build and retain a skilled work force" (Richman 1990, 76). Everyone is talking about the labor shortage, but it seems to be a matter not of shortage but of finding and keeping the right people. There are always people, but not necessarily ones that meet our needs. Once they are found, it is a matter of being able to keep them.

One company that has a good track record on both of these accounts is a medical organization that is one of the best managed in the United States: Merck & Co. Arthur F. Strohmer, executive director of Staffing and Developments, emphasizes that Merck places heavy emphasis on meeting very high standards in its recruiting activities, for example, targeting certain schools as being the "best" for the disciplines it needs. Merck, like Motorola, bases much of its campus recruiting on the past performance of employees who have come from certain schools. Many companies try to do the same thing.

Either consciously or unconsciously, companies keep returning to the same source for personnel. Whether they are truly successful or at the mercy of random selection depends on how organized they are. Many managers make choices based on assumptions rather than knowledge about which types of individuals actually do better than others. All too often the selection process is highly subjective, with applicants recognizing this and trying to play the part they need to play. Companies need some way to recruit those who are best for their particular organization. Two companies that have given systematic thought to this employee selection process are Merck and Hewlett-Packard (HP).

DIRECT COLLEGE HIRES

Almost everyone recognizes the importance of the initial interview. On the forefront of this movement is Merck. It developed a new Interview Skills Workshop, which has helped redefine the interview process.

Art Strohmer notes, "We're committed to getting the very best people, not only to fill the jobs that are open now, but to grow with us in the future" ("Skill"). He says that to find the best candidates in disciplines they need, Merck interviewers must be able to develop better skills for identifying the best.

Candidates have become increasingly sophisticated at interviewing. Some even take seminars in how to interview and how to present themselves. Merck's workshop teaches interviewers to keep control of the interview. Once education and technical qualifications of candidates have been verified, the workshop trains these managers how to isolate those job characteristics essential to perform the work.

One of Merck's interviewers, Julie Satmary, director for Accounting Standards and Training, says there are 20 or 30 personal characteristics you would like each employee to have, but in a 25-minute interview you do not have time to explore all of them. She says the course taught her to hone in on the three or four characteristics most important to a particular job, for example, the ability to work independently, to operate under close supervision, to be organized, and to resolve problems. Art Strohmer believes it is essential for Merck interviewers to understand the exact requirements for each job. He says Merck will be putting a much heavier emphasis on the development of very clear specifications for each of the jobs for which it is recruiting ("Skill"). He points out that interviewers should focus on the skills and knowledge needed to do the job effectively.

Merck's hiring process begins when the hiring managers determine what technical skills, aptitude, and behavioral characteristics will be necessary to do the job. When a candidate arrives, the hiring manager evaluates the person's technical skills. The interviewer then evaluates the behavioral or personality traits of the candidate and also tries to evaluate intangibles like interpersonal skills, motivation, initiative, leadership, and so forth.

The primary tool Merck uses to evaluate these intangibles is probing questions like: "Give me an example of a situation in which you've had to use your interpersonal skills," "How do you handle that situation?", "What was the result of your handling of the situation?", "How did you feel about the results?", "How did your coworkers feel about it?", "How did your superiors feel about it?" ("Skill").

PREPARATION

The key point with initial interviews is to plan and prepare for them. Merck helps its people prepare for interviews by conducting Interview Skills Workshops for eight to ten participants at a time. Each of these participants in the workshop engages in six mock interviews. In three of them the participant plays the role of the job applicant. In the other three each participant acts as the interviewer. Each interview is video-taped and screened so participants can observe, and hopefully improve, their own performance. During and after these mock interviews, the workshop organizers emphasize the importance of eye contact, body language, and the use of probing questions like those already mentioned.

Merck not only trains its managers how to interview but also concentrates on identifying top college and university sources of new talent within each area of expertise for which it is recruiting. Once these colleges and universities have been identified, its campus recruiting focuses its efforts on these key institutions.

To strengthen Merck's image on these critical campuses, the company invites these college placement directors and their staff to take part in a program called "A Day at Merck." These college placement individuals tour the facilities and discuss career opportunities with Merck. In a continuous effort to keep up-to-date, Merck is also creating new re-cruitment brochures and is making use of new computer software that aids prospective employees in exploring a wide range of career oppor-tunities. Merck's approach to new college hires is best summarized by Strohmer, who says its strategy is "to identify, attract and hire the top people out there; to get them early in their careers and to make sure we're getting the best people for the long-term success of the company" ("Skill").

BEHAVIORAL INTERVIEWING

Merck's goals are worthwhile, but even the best companies must con-tinuously try to improve their ability to find, keep, and maximize their people. In most cases, as with Merck, this process begins with the 30-minute interview of prospective employees. The wrong decision can and does result in turnover and thousands of dollars in training, travel, and interview time.

To help reduce this risk, many companies, like Hewlett-Packard, are using an interviewing technique called behavioral interviewing, devel-oped by organizational psychologist Paul Green. It is based on the as-sumption that past behavior is the best indicator of future behavior. Interviewers using this technique try to design questions that elicit past behavior that is closest to that needed for the job that the employee would hold.

To do behavioral interviewing, managers are expected to understand thoroughly the job requirements for prospective employees. Assuming they do understand them, they next read the resume and try to identify areas in it that need further explanation, including any weak or unclear points.

Interviewers identify the behavioral skills needed for a job. They then identify the elements of these skills to see which ones will be needed for those jobs. Behavioral interviewing identifies 21 skills that are sometimes needed on jobs. These include coping, decisiveness, assertiveness, tolerance of ambiguity, written communication skills, creativity, commitment, team building, versatility, and leadership. For each of these skills eight job behaviors help define that skill.

- have varied duties
- deal with diverse groups
- respond to others' needs
- be socially flexible
- "roll with the punches"
- understand individual differences
- make others comfortable
- exhibit wide range of social behaviors ("More" 1988)

If several of these behaviors are required for the job, then versatility is a skill needed for the applicant's job.

CHOOSING THE RIGHT QUESTIONS

Once you decide what skills are needed for a job, choose questions that will test those skills. For example, one question that Hewlett-Packard interviewers use to demonstrate a skill like versatility would be, "When was the last time you stepped out of your routine?" The interviewer asking such a question would then observe if the individual gives an example of setting aside personal preferences so as to adapt to the needs of others.

Hewlett-Packard notes that another question used by interviewers might involve asking the applicant to give an example of handling a tense situation at work. It is then up to the interviewer to decide if, in fact, the individual did cope with a tense or conflict situation. Did the individual adapt to or change the situation? ("More" 1988)

Hewlett-Packard says that once you have reviewed the behavioral skills relative to a job, you should list the technical skills that are necessary for minimum performance on the job. As with behavioral skills, create several questions to test for each of the technical skills. Be sure to have an idea of what answers are acceptable. To this end it is probably wise to try out questions on your successful workers to see how they would answer them.

Hewlett-Packard believes the behavioral interviewing approach is best because skills emerge with behavioral questions that do not emerge with the standard interview. Standard interviewers might ask a generic question like, "What do you consider to be your strong point?" Often all you get is pat answers. Interviewers at Hewlett-Packard use their behavioral skills to try to encourage candidates to give specific examples from their past that show how they have the skills needed for the job.

DECENTRALIZED HIRING

Hewlett-Packard and Merck provide some shining examples of successful, but traditional, recruiting approaches. Springfield Remanufacturing Corporation (SRC) rebuilds gasoline and diesel engines and is one of America's most successful small companies. The company has been featured on the Public Broadcasting System (PBS) special called "Growing Your Own Business." Numerous articles, including a feature article in *INC* magazine, have praised its high growth rate, outstanding quality, and leadership. Jack Stack, SRC's president, would say the critical element in its formula is its people. The company is renowned because of the way it trains and trusts its employees. Top managers give a great deal of authority to their employees, who are taught finance and responsibility and are expected to make decisions and be accountable for them.

This philosophy fits in with its hiring policy. In the early history of the company, hiring decisions were made in the traditional format, with the human resource director making all those decisions. Now the work group decides whom to hire. At SRC hiring is a group activity. No employee, past or present, has been hired or been interviewed by only one person. Gary Brown, human resource director for SRC, notes: "We all look at different things, before we accept a prospective applicant. He or she might have had as many as five or six interviews with individuals whom the applicant will work with, if they are hired."

SRC's human resource department is responsible for initial recruiting and screening of prospective employees to determine if they might fit in with the SRC philosophy. After this point the approach becomes more nontraditional. Once the human resource manager has determined that a prospective employee might fit in, in terms of work ethics, temperament, and so forth, then the prospect talks to the work group or those with whom the prospect will work. This step might involve talking to two to five people, maybe more. Later, this group gets together. One negative appraisal by any one of these people will prevent a prospective employee from working for SRC.

RECRUITMENT THROUGH REPUTATION

SRC's hiring procedures work for it but are not for everyone. In these times of labor shortages in key areas and, more importantly, skills shortages, not everyone can afford to be picky; SRC can because of its reputation as an excellent place to work. Even though the company pays only $6 or $7 an hour, it has 2,500 applicants for a plant that may have only 300 people. This overabundance of applicants occurs despite the fact that many other local industries are recruiting the same type of employee, and these companies pay considerably more. It is SRC's reputation that recruits employees. The same power of a good reputation also helps others, like Merck, which recently had 12,000 applicants for 125 sales positions.

Like other companies, SRC receives applications for employment from state employment agencies, private recruiters, and walk-in traffic. However, none of these sources provides the majority of its hires. Its most reliable source of new employees is through its own employees. There is no worry about negativism here. At SRC approximately 70 percent of new hires come from employee referrals.

If an employee wants to recommend someone for a job, the human resource department simply asks the employee to fill out a Recommend for Hire form. In essence, when SRC's employees fill out this form, they are putting their reputation and credibility on the line. The company expects its employees to use good judgment—and employees know that. Gary Brown emphasizes that "if an employee does refer a bad person, then we [SRC] will *never* take another referral from them." These employees are naturally concerned about their own reputation. As Brown comments, "If good employees recommend someone, they will not let that person fail."

MANAGING DIVERSITY

Companies like Merck, Hewlett-Packard, and SRC have done a tremendous job of creating a reputation as outstanding places to work. These reputations did not occur by accident. Each of the companies has worked hard to ensure that it gets the best applicants available.

A Boston factory called Digital Equipment Corporation may signal the hiring conditions of the future. The 350 employees at the plant come from 44 countries and speak 19 languages (Dryfuss 1990). The factory issues written announcements in English, Chinese, French, Spanish, Portuguese, Vietnamese, and Haitian Creole. Perhaps all facilities will not be this diverse, but there are significant changes occurring in the workplace.

According to the Bureau of Labor Statistics, the work force growth in the United States will slow from 2 percent between 1976 and 1988 to 1.2 percent from 1988 to 2000. More significantly, only 32 percent of the new workers will be white men. Their share of the labor force will shrink from 51 percent in 1980 to 45 percent in the future. Women will make up 47 percent of our workers, and minorities and immigrants will hold 26 percent of all jobs ("Diversity," 135). Such a diverse work culture will require greater managerial expertise.

Many of America's more progressive companies are recognizing the need for broader recruiting strategies. DuPont says that by 2025 minorities will comprise 40 percent of college-age youth ("Diversity"). The company believes this source of applicants must be effectively tapped if it is going to be able to get the needed scientists and engineers. It has already spent $1.1 million in support of aid to minority education programs at nearly 50 schools, with the goal of recruiting 45 to 50 percent of the women and minority graduates. McDonald's tries to get minorities by starting even sooner, providing summer corporate internships and year-round restaurant management programs for minority college students.

Aggressive recruitment is important, but it may come down to one's reputation. Reputation helped Merck and SRC, and the same can be said for recruitment of minorities. "Companies that don't have a reputation for a level playing field are going to have a tough time recruiting," notes Avon's CEO, James E. Preston (Dryfuss 1990). Recognizing this new reality, Hewlett-Packard managers talk to women candidates about the high rating as an employer that *Working Women* gave them. Xerox gives prospective employees reprints of a *Black Enterprise* article that rates the company as one of the best places for blacks to work. Other companies, like MacDonald's and Burger King, offer flexible hours in the hope of attracting nontraditional workers.

CHANGING ATTITUDES

Managing diversity is more than making scheduling changes; it involves a change in attitude. Greater tolerance for differences will be essential in the culture of the twenty-first century. In the near future, employees are a lot more likely to have different backgrounds. Some ethnic groups may have unorthodox styles, different values and motivation, and, most importantly, new perspectives.

DuPont is adjusting to this new perspective, but it was not always that way. Mark Suwyn, a middle-aged white male and the vice president of medical products division, noticed something. During a personal review of his department in early 1987, he noticed that women and blacks, who were highly rated when they were hired, either left the company or dropped in their ratings after a decade at the company (Maraniss

1990). He knew something was wrong, but he did not know what it was.

He knew DuPont would increasingly be made up of more black men and women and white women, so he knew he had better create an environment where they could prosper. To help investigate the problem, the company set up a "core group" composed of four white men, two black men, three white women, and one black woman. The group then met all day once or twice each month to learn how to deal with gender and race. Suwyn said he and others learned about stereotypes. Later, other cross-departmental core groups were formed in department after department. Eventually, there were eight vice presidents involved in this reassessment.

Through this and other work through a committee called Achieve Cultural Diversity, they found blacks and women were largely relegated to the lower end of the scale in performance. Several proposals were made to DuPont's leadership, which were quickly accepted. These included setting up mentoring and career development systems for both blacks and women. They also eliminated rating of one's potential for the first few years. Other departments also took black-white awareness courses.

The key to making DuPont's work force more sensitive to diversity issues was training and education ranging from basic skills training to educating the entire organization to accept more diversified behavior. In this new recruiting world, the most immediate need is for remedial education. Aetna Life, for instance, decided to train its filing, word processing, and secretarial employees after applications for clerical jobs dropped by 40 percent. Now it has classes for inner-city residents in basic office skills at its Hartford location. Applicants need to pass an aptitude test and must be able to do basic math, write a memo, and compose a business letter by the time they finish (Dryfuss 1990). Donald Stewart, president of the College Board, predicts that companies will need to shift more of their $80 billion a year on training to remedial education, including helping employees learn to read and write. Ford already spends $200 million a year in remedial and in-house training programs.

In the future, we can never assume others perceive things as we do. Never assume that they are motivated by the same needs. Sensitivity to each other's needs is essential at work where homogeneity is as unlikely as the tooth fairy. For instance, IBM recently committed $25 million to child care and elder care programs so that employees could, in the words of the chairman, John Akers, "advance their careers while minimizing the impact on their personal lives" (Bunke 1990, 7). The reason for such flexibility is that statistical companies must become more flexible and sensitive to change because the work force is changing. It has been reported that between 1990 and 2003 only 15 percent of the entrants will be white adult males. New workers will be predominantly women (60 percent), blacks, and immigrants (Bunke 1990). Thus about 30 percent of the additional work force are blacks, Hispanics, and other minorities. It will be a very different work world. In future chapters, we will look at educational and motivational strategies and techniques that enhance the effectiveness of all the work force, not just the top, not just the white, and not just the male work force.

CONCLUDING THOUGHTS

America's managers must get better—much better—at managing our diverse work culture. American business is competing with homogeneous cultures and with others that have strong work ethics. Wishful thinking accomplishes nothing. There simply is no choice. As the saying goes, "It's the hand that was dealt us."

If we manage our heterogeneous work culture properly, what many consider a liability may turn out to be our greatest opportunity. After all, diversity in experience and perception is at the heart of creativity. At least we will not end up with the same old solutions. It is extremely difficult to be creative and to see things from a different viewpoint if you have limited knowledge of other things. It is usually when you combine divergent thoughts, disciplines, or viewpoints that a totally new perspective or solution emerges.

Communicating with those who are different from us is never comfortable, but in the end, long-term solutions to our competitiveness will depend on our doing just that. In the next chapters, we will look at what can be done to find, keep, and better manage this diverse work culture.

REFERENCES

Bunke, Harvey C. "Pax Americana." *Business Horizons*, January–February, 1990, 7.

"Diversity: A Source of Strength." *DuPont* (in-house publication), 135.

Dryfuss, Joe. "Get Ready for the New Work Force." *Fortune*, April 23, 1990, 165–68.

Henkoff, Ronald. "Make Your Office More Productive." *Fortune*, February 25, 1991, 76.

Kraar, Louis. "Japan's Gung-Ho U.S. Car Plants." *Fortune*, January 30, 1989, 104.

Main, Jeremy. "The Winning Organization." *Fortune*, September 26, 1988, 56.

Maraniss, David. "Firm Makes Radical Revolution from Top Down." *Washington Post*, March 8, 1990, 1.

"More Than a Gut Feeling." *Exchange* (Hewlett-Packard in-house publication), December–January 1988, 14.

Richman, Louis S. "The Coming World Labor Shortage." *Fortune*, April 9, 1990, 76.

"The Skill of Recruiting." *Employee Relations: The Challenge Ahead* (Merck in-house publication).

3

Aggressive Recruitment for Entry-Level Workers

Organizations compete intensely for entry-level workers, especially in the food service and hotel industries. Particularly in short supply are the 16- to 24-year-olds.

Much has been said about the "baby bust." In 1984, there were approximately 24 million 16- to 24-year-olds. By 1995, that number of young adults will have shrunk to about 20 million. Also consider the fact that in 1980 young workers made up a quarter of the U.S. labor force and that by 1995, this same group will make up only 16 percent of the labor force ("Marriott").

The National Restaurant Association projects a shortfall of as many as 1 million workers in the food service industry by 1995. It is for this reason that this industry, along with the hotel industry, has been so aggressive with its recruitment methods. In particular, Marriott Corporation has been one of the most successful and aggressive organizations. Most importantly for other industries' point of view, its methods are appropriate for a wide range of industries. In the rest of this chapter we will look at some of its more successful programs.

ADOPT-A-SCHOOL

Adopt-A-School programs are national programs that create a partnership between business and schools. Sometimes these programs are called "Join-A-School." As the name implies, these programs involve a business's forming a partnership with some school. The school itself may be a high school or even an elementary school, vocational school, or university.

The main value of an Adopt-A-School program is that it helps establish a closer relationship with a particular school. In the process you create a better understanding of your business and industry.

There are some solid reasons for such a program. As we shall see, it helps make it easier to recruit some personnel, it can improve your image and increase the chance that some choose your business as a career, and it increases the chance of creating a broader labor pool.

In this process, you also help improve the U.S. educational system, the point being that "if you are not part of the solution, then you're part of the problem." When you participate in the Adopt-A-School program, you are part of the educational solution because you help strengthen school programs. In the process you help both the school and the community be better prepared for the future.

Getting involved in an Adopt-A-School program requires a commitment of one year during which you basically "adopt" a school and develop a relationship with the school and its students.

When establishing an Adopt-A-School program, make sure you gain the support and commitment of the key managers of the corporation. You must also gain the support and commitment of those who must implement the program. Without the support of both of these groups, little will happen.

Once you have achieved the support of management and those who must give their time and effort, then and only then should you make a commitment to local schools. Unless you provide 100 percent support for the program, there is no reason to do it.

Actual participation in Adopt-A-School involves developing a series of projects and programs that allow you and a school to interact with each other. One of these projects should be to make sure your key people speak to the school on a regular basis. Efforts should also be made to be an active, rather than a passive, partner, for example, by seeking to broaden the students' experience and increasing the relevance of their curriculum. Focus your efforts on those things that are of greatest importance to you and future employees, like the need for better written communication, math, science skills, and so on. Additional ways to get involved include offering incentives and prizes to the school's best students and arranging field trips to your organization.

MARRIOTT'S PROGRAM

Marriott has enhanced its ability to recruit and retain employees through the Adopt-A-School program. Each organization runs its Adopt-A-School program differently, but Marriott begins by hosting a two-day seminar called "A Workshop with Professionals" for high school students of its Edison Career Vocational Center at corporate headquarters

(Stephens, 11). At these workshops the staff at the center speaks to the students about various aspects of the food service industry.

Each Marriott approaches its Adopt-A-School program somewhat differently. Marriott, for instance, actively recruits and develops new personnel at its Sheridan Vocational Technical Center. Tim Krajewski, executive chef at the Fort Lauderdale Beach Marriott, said, "We have hosted receptions at our hotel for their faculty, visited their school for lunch, held career day/job fairs at our hotel as well as shadowing by their students, to give them a perspective in how a hotel kitchen operates" (Stephens, 11).

Krajewski went on to say that the Sheridan Vocational Technical Centers have proven very successful. In fact, six of the graduating students from the Sheridan Center are employed in his kitchen.

Another of Marriott's centers focuses on practical training for hospitality students at the George C. Marshall High School. In this program 15 students from the high school report to work at various areas between 7:30 A.M. and 9:00 A.M., Wednesday through Friday. This program has been very successful. Marriott gets free labor, and many of these students eventually work part-time after school and on weekends.

The benefits of such programs are not one-sided. Students gain critical work experience, since they move through different positions within the Marriott facility. They can also hone their job skills, because student performance is then evaluated by Marriott's staff and an instructor who is on the property at all times. Thus, they are allowed to make mistakes and correct them before their job and career depend on their performance.

PRACTITIONERS AS TEACHERS

Marriott's participation with high school work programs is designed to meet its needs and help high school students gain experience and consider careers in the hotel field, and the company makes use of other programs designed to influence students' career choices.

One particularly effective program was explained by Paul Puzzanhero, food and beverage director at Marriott's Boston Long Wharf. He said, "We have begun a program with Boston University Hotel and Restaurant Curriculum to teach a one-credit elective course within their Hotel and Restaurant School" (Stevens, 11).

The course is taught five times a semester for two hours each time. Puzzanhero said that Marriott was able to teach the course by convincing Boston University's director of Marriott's educational programs and that Marriott could make a positive contribution to students' education. He emphasized the hands-on nature of the course, in which Marriott provides professionals to teach the principles of food and beverage in hotel work.

The goal of the course from Marriott's viewpoint (besides providing quality instruction to students) is to have these students become more familiar with Marriott. The hope is that when these students seek part- or full-time work, they will consider working for Marriott. In fact, many part-timers were recruited to work evenings and weekends. These students, in turn, helped reduce some of the labor shortage at the hotel.

Marriott increases the effectiveness of the program by providing an incentive in the form of a scholarship of $1,000 to the outstanding student of the year. The money comes from the $750 teaching fee plus $250 that Marriott contributed. Public relations for its efforts were also enhanced by publication of the winner in the school's paper.

LONG-TERM SOLUTIONS

Marriott's local hotel staff have become involved in Adopt-A-School programs in high schools, junior colleges, and universities, thereby providing an opportunity for solving their labor shortages. Though the program is not of immediate help in solving labor shortages, Marriott hotels have even become involved with elementary schools.

Obviously, working with elementary schools does not immediately help to alleviate its labor shortage, but there are advantages. Marriott believes such association helps provide a long-term solution to students not choosing careers in its field. For this reason it makes use of several school-related activities, one of which is career days.

CAREER DAYS

A business's exposure to students during school career days is a way to encourage students to choose a particular industry or job as a career. Related to these career days is a program that Marriott's Washington, DC metropolitan area calls "FREE," which stands for Find and Recruit Excellent Employees. FREE consists of several programs, including one to get high school students to have a better appreciation of careers in their area.

To kick off the FREE program, Marriott held a reception in the Washington, DC, area involving high school counselors, university and college placement directors, government agencies, and minority organizations. The purpose of this reception was twofold: to tell these referral sources about career opportunities in their area and to educate these referral groups about the kind of applicant for whom hotels are looking.

These goals were accomplished by holding a reception in one of the area's hotel's meeting rooms. Around the room were various booths manned by both hourly and management personnel. Each of these booths represented a different job in the hotel, including housekeeping, front desk clerk, waiter, chef, and so on. After this initial orientation, a formal reception was held. At this reception, various Marriott executives discussed topics such as career opportunities, the company's culture, and the kind of people it wants to hire. All of these activities were followed by a question-and-answer period.

Formal programs like this one can be of invaluable aid to recruiting people but by no means exhaust your vehicles for aggressive recruiting. Student groups are one such tool that most managers have not fully explored. Trudy Mariotta, a representative for Marriott in the Bethesda, Maryland, area, works with two such school-based organizations—Future Homemakers of America (FHA) and the Distributive Education Clubs of America (DECA). The long-term goal is to interest students in careers in the hospitality industry (Fintel).

Marriott works with these two organizations as part of its work-study arrangement with various high schools in the area. The reason it goes to such efforts is simple: when these students need a job, they are more likely to think of Marriott simply because they are familiar with the company.

FHA

The Future Homemakers of America has a national membership of 325,000 men and women in 12,000 chapters.[1] FHA's goal is to encourage personal growth leadership as well as family and community involvement. Primarily, FHA chapters explore home economics–related jobs and careers.

Some newer chapters of FHA also emphasize *preparation* for jobs and careers in home economics–related occupations (HERO). These HERO chapters are essentially the male counterpart of the older FHA.

DECA

A less-known high school student organization is the Distributive Education Clubs of America.[2] DECA consists of high school students who are interested in various careers in marketing, distribution, merchandising, and management. DECA is designed to be used as part of normal classroom instructional activities. It has two objectives: to further educate students in marketing, distribution, merchandising, and management careers and to promote an understanding of citizenship in a free competitive enterprise. Generally, DECA tries to develop not only a vocational understanding necessary to compete in these careers but also students' self-confidence, self-esteem, ethical standards, and communication skills.

Marriott has been a corporate sponsor of DECA and is even on its National Advisory Board and has served as judges at local and national competitions.

JUNIOR ACHIEVEMENT

Junior Achievement (JA) is the United States' oldest educational organization, funded by the business community and private foundations. JA includes the JA high school program, Project Business, Business Basics, and Applied Economics. Project Business is an enrichment program for junior high school students. Basic Business is at the elementary level, and the Applied Economics is a new classroom program for high school students. Those JA programs most applicable to business are the high school program and Project Business.

The high school program is called the JA Company Program. In this program, student members, with guidance from adult volunteer advisers, form groups of approximately 20 members. Each of these groups then functions as a small business and meets one night each week for about two and one-half hours. Typically, in such meetings the students sell stock and choose a product to produce or service to provide. They also keep their books and marketing plans, pay salaries, produce products, promote them, and so forth. At the end of the school term they liquidate their company, publish an annual report, and provide returns on dividends to stockholders.[3]

PROJECT BUSINESS

Project Business is a a 10- to 12-week economic education program that helps eighth and ninth graders understand business and economics. In this program, business consultants, on a weekly basis, share firsthand experience on the U.S. economic system. They also review other topics like supply and demand, the marketplace, and financial, personal, and global economics. Although it is not necessary for a consultant to address all of these topics, many are usually discussed in the classroom and through field trips to local businesses. Marriott found that a weekly commitment of two hours is advisable, including one hour per week in the classroom and one hour to prepare for the class.[4]

OLDER WORKERS

As young workers become increasingly scarce, older, more mature people offer an opportunity for employers; they also provide a special challenge. Many employers cannot afford to ignore this challenge since meeting the older person's requirements will be necessary as labor shortages occur and the general population continues to age. Despite the need to maximize this resource, older people continue to be an untapped resource.

There are several reasons companies are hiring older workers. Studies have shown that customers prefer to deal with older workers and go out of their way to be served by them (Stephens, 11). Furthermore, these older workers tend to be more responsible, trustworthy, and productive.

Marriott works very hard at recruiting and retaining these older workers. The reasons are simple: Marriott reports that these older workers have less absenteeism and a greater sense of responsibility for the company than do many younger workers and are more careful and experience fewer accidents.

On the downside, Marriott reports that older people are sometimes reluctant to turn to the food service for employment. It also notes that recruitment for older employees does not work well when using the traditional methods, like radio, television, and even newspaper advertising.

Because of the limited value of traditional recruitment tools when seeking older employees, Marriott suggests additional efforts be made, like developing clear and definitive statements concerning all aspects of employment. Other suggestions include using senior citizen groups at churches or at community centers. The American Association of Retired Persons (AARP) in Washington, DC, also advises putting up notices in laundromats, convenience stores, and centers where free or discounted meals are served.

When describing jobs for older people and when setting up work schedules, Marriott suggested you consider the following:

- provide explicit details about the openings, job descriptions, and other details about the jobs
- identify job requirements and employment conditions
- provide clear information on wages, benefits, and flexible work options (older workers generally prefer part-time work)

MINORITIES

In this age of diversity, the decrease in white male workers and the corresponding increase in available minorities and working women make it imperative that we recruit and retain this population. One place to find them is through the Urban League, which provides special skill-training programs, counseling, and job placement. The Urban League is designed to help African-Americans. In various communities, there are similar Vietnamese, Mexican-American, or other minority associations that can be used to locate and help train untapped labor.

Additionally, employers who wish to recruit minorities can contact centers where English is a second language. You can also use community centers, youth centers, and churches. For example, at a Domino's Pizza Store in Silver Springs, Maryland, Manager Mike Murray says two of his best employees were referred to him by the Church of Latter-Day Saints. The Mormon church has its own employment services with about 70 branches. An additional bonus is that you do not have to pay for their services.

DISABLED EMPLOYEES

The Americans with Disabilities Act states that, as employers, we should all focus more on finding and hiring disabled workers. Marriott makes excellent use of this employee resource by employing more than 6,000 disabled people. Its philosophy is that if individuals are properly trained, supported, and matched with a job, then they can do an excellent job.

USING AGENCIES

You can always use the government to help you find employees; actually, there is quite a bit that government agencies can provide. The Private Industry Council (PIC) Training Programs can help you with staffing problems. PIC and other government agencies require a written outline of your training program to assure that their applicants have the opportunity to attain marketable skills.

There is a certain amount of reimbursement for training cost, provided you have hired people through the Job Training Partnership Act (JTPA) agencies. These include PIC, the Council of Governments, Alliance of Business, Catholic churches, and the Refugee Assistance Association.

Goodwill Industries can also provide an excellent source of job referrals. Roy Rogers restaurants in Washington, DC, have made excellent use of these services. If you use Goodwill, then its representatives will go through your training program and return to their local agencies to screen applicants. These Goodwill representatives then work with new employees until they develop the competence needed to do their job.

The Alliance of Business can also provide a listing of organizations in your community for placing the hard to employ, including refugees, handicapped, and welfare recipients. Agencies that employ temporary help are also a source for those wanting to enter the work force.

In general, other activities Marriott says can increase retention and recruitment include making yourself visible and accessible to the community. In addition to those techniques already mentioned, use brochures and fliers as a marketing tool to community, high schools, and colleges. You might also consider filling part-time positions by working with other local employers who need to fill jobs on alternating schedules, for example, local maintenance companies that employ workers for early morning and late evening.

CONCLUDING THOUGHTS

As you can see, there are many alternatives if a company is aggressive about its recruiting efforts. It is a matter of deciding what types of entry-level employee you want and choosing some of these or other recruiting tools. The point is to think creatively and not use the same old resources. Experimentation will eventually lead to a process that best suits your needs.

NOTES

1. If you would like to obtain more information about the FHA, you can write to the following address: Future Homemakers of America, Inc., 1910 Association Drive, Reston, VA 22091.

2. If you would like more information about DECA, then contact: Frederick L. Willford, Ph.D., Executive Director, Distributive Education Clubs of America, 1908 Association Drive, Reston, VA 22091.

3. If interested in volunteering to be one of these advisers, you can contact Junior Achievement, which is listed in the white pages of the telephone book.

4. If you want to get more involved in Project Business or JA activities, then contact: Junior Achievement, Inc., Communication Department, 550 Summer Street, Stamford, CT 06901.

REFERENCES

"Marriott Corporation: High School Awareness Program." *Inside Marriott* (Marriott news and information report).
Stephens, Sam. "Yes, I Can Make a Difference in the Labor Crisis." *Acclaim* 11.

4

What's Going on in Academia?

When recruiting employees and managers, a business should ask, "Are we getting our money's worth?" In a recent article in *Business Week*, Richard R. West, the dean of New York University's Graduate School of Business, relates a frightening conversation he had with a group of management faculty in his office. West asked them a simple question, "Could Peter Drucker get tenure here today?" Surprisingly, the faculty said no, that he would not deserve tenure, even though he was once a tenured professor at the school.

As hard as it is to believe, Drucker, the management guru, would not get tenure if it were up to those faculty members. Their reason was simple enough: they perceived him as a journalist, not a scholar (Bryne 1990). This incident would not be so discouraging if their attitude were unique, but it is a commonly held bias.

Six years after this incident West, along with a lot of others inside and outside academia, believes things are not right. In fact, such attitudes seem to have worsened. West says he is amazed by what he considers the overemphasis placed on scholarly research at most business schools (Bryne 1990). He said that if he were writing a book, it would be on the bankruptcy of American management education!

Bankruptcy—maybe. Pompous, pretentious, and surely irrelevant—most undoubtedly. Colleges of business administration (COBAs) are not what many practitioners think they are. Those on the outside mistakenly think teaching at business schools is the top priority. Most people, including business leaders, do not realize how colleges have changed.

SECOND-CLASS STATUS

The plain truth is that teaching has become less and less important to business schools and perhaps to university education in general. The demise of teaching as a focus of business schools started in the 1950s when the Ford and Carnegie Foundation helped redirect business education. At that time business schools were mostly vocational. To gain respect, schools lured intellectuals to their faculties. Business education got better—but somewhere along the line, teaching got lost in the shuffle. In their quest for research and research money, business schools lost the desire and ability to teach.

Today, as an article in the *U.S. News and World Report* emphasized, "so many campuses have been transformed into mammoth research centers, a disturbing proportion of the faculty come to look upon classroom teaching the way secretaries look at filing" (Elfin 1990, 104). No one says it openly, but in fact most business professors do not like to teach and find students a nuisance. Students just get in their way of doing more enjoyable things like research.

The vast majority of professors do not have the basic skills to teach. Even if they wanted to teach, and most do not, they do not know how. Most believe that knowing about a specialized area and simply talking about the subject or, more importantly, talking about their "research" are teaching. Those same thoughts were expressed by Robert Rosenzweig, president of the Association of American Universities, an association of 58 major research universities. He said: "For too long, universities led by the best of them dealt with it (this neglect of undergraduates) by asserting that simply being in the frontier of their field was beneficial to students. That sometimes seems to be little more than being in the same city with them" (Elfin 1990, 104).

We are not asking them to be great teachers, only good ones. Ralph Benke and Roger Hermanson provide some simple advice for those who want to be better teachers. They say that professors could:

1. spend considerable time planning and organizing their course . . . and to emphasize expectations and flexibility,
2. make a special effort to become aware of individual traits and interest of their students (and have a positive regard for them),
3. ask questions of the class, encourage questions and move around the classroom, and finally,
4. communicate with students through written comments on exams and papers, as well as give them praise and recommend specific learning alternatives (Benke and Hermanson 1990, 561).

That is simple advice. It may not be earth-shattering, but it would surely make many of our business professors a lot more relevant. Anemic teaching skills and desires are not the only signs of irrelevance in higher education.

"IT'S ONLY ACADEMIC"

How many times have you heard, "It's only academic"? When I hear that statement, someone is usually referring to the fact that the focus of the discussion is on irrelevant matters. Can we really afford education in today's competitive environment that is irrelevant or at least not meeting our needs? No better example of this irrelevance is seen than with faculty research. It seems we should expect a lot from faculty research. After all, we gave up good teaching so faculty could focus on their research.

In today's business school even when faculty do research, its usefulness is doubtful and benefits dubious. Many professors do not even care if it is irrelevant. They simply hide under the blanket of "basic" research. They seem to take great pride in the fact that basic research is justification enough. The question is, do taxpayers, business consumers, and the American economy really need another survey of college students or even the formulation of another managerial theory— or instead do they need help to solve our competitive and productive problems?

Business Week reports that critics say professors are spending too much time on fuzzy academic theories in narrowly defined disciplines (Bryne 1990). Scott S. Cowen, dean of the Weatherhead School of Management at Case Western Reserve University, notes, "As much as 80 percent of management research may be irrelevant" (Bryne 1990, 62).

If things are to get better, we have to ask, Are we getting our money's worth? Passive business spending is to blame in large part for the lack of relevance in business research. *Fortune* magazine reported that in 1988 business spent $2.1 billion (that's over $2,000 million!) on education. Ninety percent of that money went to universities and vocational schools (Dumaine 1990). Millions of dollars go into business research, but what are we getting for that money? Since the bulk of it goes to support faculty who want to do something other than teach, the question seems like a reasonable one.

IT'S A MATTER OF PRIORITIES

Stanford president, Donald Kennedy, bluntly summarized the situation in most schools when he said: "Junior faculty who show outstanding teaching ability fail to achieve the tenure line too often, to the dismay of students who understandably wonder about Stanford's values. It is time to reaffirm that education, that is, teaching in all its forms, is the primary task" (Toch 1990, 107).

J. Dennis Huston of Rice University, named by the Carnegie Foundation for the Advancement of Teaching as the 1989 Professor of the Year, says the truth is that writing is the way to become rich, to make a name (Dumaine 1990). So professors view time spent away from publishing as wasteful. Teaching does not bring job offers; publishing a book does. When we change the reward structure, we will change the structure of education.

Teaching loads have shrunk to allow more time for research. School administrators talk about the need for good teachers but in the next breath recruit researchers. Unfortunately many, if not most, of the researchers do not like to teach; they like to do research. All too often not all research is of equal merit. It is only so-called scholarly works that are considered appropriate for university researchers.

HBR—WHORING?

Coming from a technical discipline, I had always thought that creating or transmitting relevant and practical information was a noble calling. It as only when I became exposed to business schools that I began to realize that one might "look down" on vocational or applied knowledge. Absurd, you might think, but it is true.

The stars of business schools are the scholars, not the practitioners. In fact, if you write for practitioners rather than scholars, you are seen as somewhat of a second-class citizen. This attitude was succinctly described by John W. Roseblum, dean of the University of Virginia's Darden School, who said that most academics look down on well-read journals like the *Harvard Business Review* (*HBR*). When asked what academics would think of writing for *HBR*, he said, "It's not quite whoring, but if it's given any value, it's seen as educational instead of scholarly" (Bryne 1990, 62). Roseblum said that such an attitude was unfortunate. Unfortunate, indeed—absurd is more like it. Can you imagine that writing that is relevant enough to be of interest to general business readers is somehow less appropriate? If *HBR* is almost whoring, are *Fortune, Time, Newsweek*, and other popular magazines whoring?

With such an attitude among many academics, is it possible it could get any worse? You bet! Because of the continuing failure of the American high school educational process, students are coming to college less and less prepared. Also, with the decentralization of management, empowerment of employees, and the demands placed on the organization because of worldwide competition, a better-trained work force is essential. Indeed, as *U.S. News and World Report* notes, college teaching has hit bottom just as higher education faces the herculean challenge of coping with the increasingly ill-prepared and poorly motivated products of the nation's high schools (Toch 1990, 107).

Talk to teachers at the junior high schools and elementary schools, and you will find the ability of these kids is not getting better. The environment for learning is getting worse. Broken homes, lack of parental involvement, drugs, and neglect are all taking their toll. Tamar March, academic dean at Hobart and William Smith Colleges in Geneva, said it best when he pointed out, "Now more than ever students need to be teased out of their indifference to learning" (Toch 1990, 107). American business needs teachers—not Ph.D.'s of research. We need real answers, not irrelevant theories, and we need them now!

AACSB

To understand what can be done, we must first recognize those forces that have created the current situation. There are many, but perhaps two of the biggest reasons down to two organizations. Surprisingly, one of these is the accreditation agency for business schools called the American Assembly of Collegiate Schools of Business (AACSB).

The AACSB is the self-regulating agency for colleges of business. Its membership is composed primarily of deans of the colleges of business. Most colleges of business administration (COBA) that are not members of the AACSB are trying to become members of the organization because membership brings greater status and recognition within the academic community.

The AACSB uses a variety of criteria to judge whether a business school should be admitted or whether a current member can renew membership. Each school applying or reapplying for membership is visited by an AACSB team. Members of these teams use both objective and subjective criteria to make sure that prospective schools meet their standards. These standards cover a wide range of subjects, including the number of Ph.D.'s teaching courses, support for faculty, and so forth. In theory they look at everything and are very thorough, but the key criterion is the schools' published research and writing by full-time faculty.

It is impossible to get the AACSB to state the significance of this research over other criteria. However, most administrators who are being evaluated by the AACSB know that the basis for admission to, or continued membership in, the AACSB is the quality and quantity of academic research.

Any school applying for membership knows that in the past only one type of research has been considered appropriate: theoretical or empirical "discovery" research. Such basic research is not necessarily expected to have any relevance. For most academic researchers this is the only true research; everything else is journalism (thus the comment about Peter Drucker). Applied research, which seeks to transfer knowledge or to solve competitive, productive, or quality problems, would be classified as illegitimate research.

WHO IS A PEER?

Only very recently some members within the AACSB have recognized that perhaps—just perhaps—their definition was a bit limited. Maybe such things as writing teaching cases, creating computer software, and even writing textbooks and other pedagogical work might also be considered legitimate research. The trouble is that most in academia do not really believe things are changing. There is no proof, no tangible evidence, that things might be changing. Therefore, no one in business education really believes anything is changing or will change. Sometimes people say one thing and act another way.

While business-related research would seem to be a natural type of research for business schools, it rarely occurs. It might be that academics are simply more interested in determining statistical significance rather than relevance. Perhaps these Ph.D.'s simply do not know how to do relevant research. It is much easier to focus on statistical analysis than worry about relevance. It is this type of analysis, not relevance, that is taught when future Ph.D.'s do their dissertations.

The resistance to change could also be because, within the academic community, there is little perceived need for change. According to the AACSB, research must be "written, be subject to scrutiny and criticism by one's peers and extend the boundaries of current knowledge" (Toch 1990, 107).

It sounds like a noble objective; the only trouble with the definition is that the word *peer* has a very limited meaning for academics. For most of those in academia the word *peer* does not mean practitioner; it certainly is not an editor of any number of popular or trade magazines. In fact, some, as noted earlier, might call that work whoring. Generally, a peer from an academic standpoint is one who is highly specialized and narrowly focused and appealing to a limited audience.

THE TRUE CULPRIT?

So how have things become so disjointed? The answer in part lies in business schools and the AACSB's perception of itself. In a report on research and its relevance, the authors of an AACSB report note, "The hiring market affords the best mechanism for ensuring that the change in relative supply meets the change in relative demand" (Jacobs, Reinmuth, and Hamada 1987, 4). Translation: if we (business schools) are not doing our job, then the hiring market (business organizations) will let us know—so do not worry about it!

The AACSB Task Force says, "The hiring market thus subsumes any role the AACSB might otherwise need to play in ensuring that business faculties will engage in research which ultimately improves the practice of management" (Jacob, Reinmuth, and Hamada 1987, 4). It is always hard to understand an academic, but it sounds as if the AACSB is saying that determining relevance is not up to them but rather up to employers to choose if what colleges teach are relevant; if not, then they should not hire these students if the business school's performance is not relevant.

Even if you believe you know what is relevant, academics are not so sure you know! In fact, the AACSB is not even sure that information obtained from direct interviews with managers about the relevance of faculty research is valid. The agency says these interviews can be misleading and counterproductive for two reasons: small samples are taken, and, in the terms of AACSB, there is "no single type of research that is optimally beneficial for all managers, all graduates and all schools" (Jacob, Reinmuth, and Hamada 1987, 4).

In the end, the AACSB comes back to its key point that the best indicator of the value of academic research is the hiring market. As the authors of the task force on research note, "If what the research business faculty do is, in fact, relevant to improving the practice of management, the hiring market for business graduates will reflect that over time" (Jacob, Reinmuth, and Hamada 1987, 4). They may be right. It is a fact that since 1970, business enrollments have doubled and reversed a tendency to hire liberal arts graduates instead of business graduates.

The important point is, Does the AACSB's logic make sense? For many this logic smacks of a cop-out. After all, where is business going to go to hire people if it does not go to business schools? Many, wrongly or rightly, believe that an ill-prepared business graduate is better than a liberal arts graduate who has no training in business. Besides, it does not seem to make sense that whether or not the market hires business school graduates has any connection with the relevance of faculty research. Preparation for a job has more to do with teaching and training than with a professor's research interests.

A CLOSED SOCIETY

Indeed, the logic in the idea that the relevance of business research lies in the graduates hired is curious. AACSB is an almost exclusively closed society. It is composed primarily of deans of business schools. One would have to look long and hard to find a practitioner at one of its meetings. It seems odd that, despite business colleges being the supplier, the AACSB does not have direct and continuous involvement with those who will do the hiring.

The AACSB's arm's-length approach toward practitioners is fairly typical of colleges of business. Many business schools have almost no contact with business leaders. Some COBAs do make use of "advisory councils" composed of local business leaders.

The name may apply that these councils actively advise COBAs, but the role is usually much different. For example, consider one dean who said she wanted to create an advisory council. The faculty, fearing infringement, cringed at the thought. The dean reassured the faculty, "We want their money, not their advice."

BUSINESS APATHY

Can you really blame academicians for their apathy? After all, who wants to change? What does seem to be at fault is business apathy. In 1984, the AACSB commissioned a strategic study of the future of management education. In essence, the principal findings included the following:

- Within universities and their business schools there is little perceived need for major changes in the way in which collegiate management education is carried out. Complacency and self-satisfaction appear to be the dominant attitudes in many schools.
- The corporate world is generally satisfied with business school performance. Managers and executives applaud the analytical skills, motivation, and content area knowledge of business graduates. However, they would like to see more "realistic, practical, hands-on" education with greater emphasis on the development of "people" (e.g., leadership/interpersonal) skills (Porter and McKibbin, 1).

The report says that corporate response to the survey supports the idea that research should be one of the missions of university business schools but that business pays little attention to this research. The academic community believes the AACSB and its accrediting process have contributed positively to the quality of education, but it recognizes that business itself pays little attention to the quality of business education. Whether or not academics care about the fact that their research is irrelevant to potential users is another matter. The report also says that most recognize that academics and corporate managers do not interact enough.

SO WHAT CAN BE DONE?

Our current problems with irrelevant business research and a lack of emphasis on teaching are not the fault of the AACSB. They probably are not really the fault of the Ph.D.'s. Many chose to become college professors because they wanted to do research, not teach. Such programs do not even teach Ph.D.'s how to teach, only how to do research. They are never made to understand teaching's relevance. A highly educated work force is essential to our need for empowered workers, to our competitiveness. Entry-level managers and college graduates will be essential.

The ultimate responsibility for our current educational flaws must rest with business and employers. Until business decides enough is enough, nothing will change. After all, business pays millions upon millions of dollars to support business schools. Business leaders have allowed themselves to be treated with neglect. They pay the bills but expect little in return. Until business organizes and demands changes in the quality of the educational services it consumes, little change will occur.

RECOMMENDATIONS FOR CHANGE

The first recommendation to get a higher-quality educational product is a simple one, namely, start advising. If you or your organization advises business schools, then stop advising and start advocating. Business must start demanding accountability for a better-educated product. Remember the dean who wants your money but not your advice? Do not let that happen! Ask yourself, Are you a satisfied customer?

Be aggressive about expectations. Find ways of measuring the delivery of educational services, then expect improvement of that delivery. Earlier, we noted that businesspeople would like graduates to have better human relations skills. The solution is to not hire graduates until you are convinced that the school curriculum and teachers are delivering these skills. Look hard and find a school that delivers what you want or is willing to change. Thus, the recommendation:

Business, acting as the customer, must organize and become actively involved in demanding management accountability, responsibility, and relevance to today's competitive environment.

The second recommendation also involves business support for teaching. If business supported teaching the way it does university research, there would be no teaching program. Business leaders need to support teaching by providing incentives and recognition for professors or colleges that provide exceptional teaching.

Before recruiting, business leaders need to measure results, talk to students, and evaluate inventiveness, teaching innovation, and dedication to students. Do not hire students from schools that do not have a large supply of outstanding teachers. If a school does not have outstanding teachers, then demand mandatory training programs to help them become better teachers.

Most importantly, business leaders must assume the responsibility to audit the quality of teaching their potential employees will receive. Businesses have certified suppliers; why not certified educational suppliers? Companies today are working in close cooperation with their suppliers to provide more competitive, high-grade products and services. Why not do the same with education?

Like other suppliers, education should not be a "black box," but it has been treated that way in the past. Organizations should not simply go to campuses to recruit fresh new employees. It seems much more logical that business recruiters find out what is going on in the schools' classes. It will take longer, but you can never expect to improve the consistency of the educational product you buy if you have to rely on a 30-minute interview.

Business recruiters need specifically to find out what the students are learning and how they are being taught, not what they say they are being taught. In today's competitive marketplace it seems remarkably out-of-date to expect a customer to buy a product or service without fully understanding it, but that situation is exactly what happens with education. When businesses do not fully audit educational services as they would any product or service they buy, they do both themselves and their suppliers an injustice.

Would you continue to buy a product from your supplier if that supplier refused to make the necessary changes to meet your needs? Suppose the supplier, like an educational supplier, resisted change? What would you do? Most would find one or a few suppliers, develop close relationships with them, and guarantee to do business only with them. Thus the second recommendation is:

Develop a certified educational supplier institution where the attitude is that of partnership between supplier (e.g., COBA) and you, the customer.

The purpose of a proposal for a certified educational supplier, as well as of other suggestions, is for education to be relevant. There should be, but often is not, a strong relationship between the teaching of academic subjects and real-life applications, rather than memorizing formulas and text material. Future employees must be taught how to make decisions and how to solve problems. They need to know how to learn and how to think. They need to start tasks and take them all the way through to completion. Students need to learn teamwork, cooperation, and working with people.

Educational preparation is too important to leave to just business school professors or academic deans. Business leaders and teachers most jointly set educational requirements for future employees. Students, teachers, and business employers must fully understand what is expected of employee and employer.

More than ever before, we need industry input to help set educational requirements for new personnel. There is no best plan. Some have suggested that American education needs more apprenticeships like those that already exist in the construction industry. Others, like Hoechst Celanese Corporation, have formed an internship where teachers stay two weeks at their company and are paired with a mentor who supervises their work ("Three" 1988). Still others suggest that all college students should be required to participate in cooperative educational programs where students spend part of their college time working with real managers, solving real problems. Regardless of the form, greater partnership needs to be forged. Thus our third recommendation is:

Form active partnerships with business schools and promote reforms so educational institutions are more relevant.

The final recommendation concerns research, rather than teaching. Business is increasingly being asked to help fund business research. A survey of companies by *Fortune* magazine found that 80 percent of the companies surveyed give to colleges or universities. Graduate schools and high schools come next ("Three" 1988). According to the article, only 6 percent of those corporations believe their involvement made any differences.

Too few practitioners challenge the relevance of what they are paying for. Unfortunately, many businesspeople mistakenly assume, like students, that Ph.D.'s are just too smart to understand. If their research relevance cannot be clearly explained to laymen, then the businessperson should not fund it. Demand that Ph.D.'s make their research understandable. Thus our last recommendation is:

Business organizations should not subsidize specialized faculty research of debatable quality and relevance.

CONCLUDING THOUGHTS

The competitive advantage in today's marketplace is clearly the application and advances in educating an increasingly skilled and college-educated work force. Learning in school and learning on the job are by far the most important factors accounting for America's economic growth and productivity in this century. It has been noted that between 1929 and 1982 education prior to work was responsible for 26 percent of the expansion in the nation's productive capacity (Denison 1985). Learning on the job contributed over half (about 55 percent) of all improvements in the nation's productive capacity (Carnevale 1989).

Education is extremely important to America's future. It has never been more important. Businesses change because competition forces them, but educational institutions do not change without outside pressure. Business leaders must be forceful and clear about what they want, push colleges for the necessary change, and support those that do change.

REFERENCES

Benke, Ralph, Jr., and Robert H. Hermanson. "Be a Better Teacher." *Management Accounting* 71 (April 1990): 561.

Bryne, John. "Is Research in the Ivory Tower Fuzzy, Irrelevant, Pretentious?" *Business Week*, October 29, 1990, 62.

Carnevale, Anthony P., and Leila J. Gainer. *The Learning Enterprise*. U.S. Department of Labor Employment and Training Administration. February 1989, 3.

Denison, E. F. *Trends in American Economic Growth 1929–1982*. Washington, DC: Brookings Institution, 1985.

Dumaine, Brian. "Making Education Work." *Fortune* (Special Issue), Spring 1990, 12.

Elfin, Mel. "Getting Back to Basics." *U.S. News and World Report*, October 15, 1990, 104.

Jacob, Nancy L., James E. Reinmuth, and Robert S. Hamada. *Final Report on the AACSB Task Force on Research*, January 1987, 4.

Porter, Lyman W., and Lawrence E. McKibbin. "Management Education and Development: Drift or Thrust into the 21st Century." *Executive Summary*.

"Three Teachers Hit the Labs." *Reporter* 2, no. 3 (December 1988): 6.

Toch, Thomas. "A Return to Teaching." *U.S. News and World Report*, October 15, 1990, 107.

5

Keeping Employees

It is hard to find good people. Naturally, once you find them, it is essential to find ways to keep them. One company that has done just that is Federal Express. The world's largest cargo airline has big numbers, like $5 billion in revenues. It also has some impressive small numbers, like a staff turnover rate of around 1 percent (Trunick 1989).

We learn from Federal Express that retention is interrelated with recruitment and employee relations. Each impacts the other, and all three are related. If you are careful whom you recruit, then there is a better match between recruits and company and you are more likely to retain them. Federal Express begins its retention efforts by centralizing its recruitment efforts.

Federal Express has recruitment centers in 25 locations nationwide to provide better-quality applicants for managers to interview. All screening of applicants is handled by the recruitment centers, which work under the direction of regional personnel offices. At each of these centers a peer recruiter program was introduced to help professional recruiters process and screen applicants. As the name implies, these peer recruiters have actual experience with the type of work that recruits will perform. Not only do these peer recruiters help select recruits, but job applicants receive a more realistic insight about what is expected of them and their positions.

AFTER HIRING

While good recruitment is certainly important, undoubtedly what occurs to recruits after joining the company determines whether a company will be able to retain them. When Fred Smith, the CEO of Federal Express, was asked about its success, he said, "I don't think a damn thing Federal Express does in terms of its people is particularly revolutionary and unknown." So what differentiates it from other companies and makes it so effective? Smith answered this question by gesturing to the books surrounding him on his office shelves and said, "We just do what's in all those books" (Trunick 1989, 19).

Federal Express takes managerial theory and effectively translate it into action through a philosophy defined as "people, service, profits." The company points out that it is no accident that *people* are listed first in the phrase. Federal Express says placing people first makes good business sense. Everything good that occurs is based on your ability to involve your people.

Perhaps it is because of Federal Express's attitude that it has been union-free since its inception in 1973. As recently as October 1989, union representation was rejected by the company's flight crew members. Few carriers can make such a statement.

So what has led to these good employee relations? It is not talk, but rather deeds that impress employees and improve relations. Smith notes, "I think a lot of companies talk about how their employees are their most important asset, but where you can really tell whether it is very important or not is how much their senior management spends on the issues" (Trunick 1989, 19). He says that he spends about 25 percent of his time on personnel issues, probably five times what the average CEO spends on those issues.

Implementing the "people, service, profits" philosophy comes by answering several basic questions. The first is, What is expected of me, and what do you want me to do? Federal Express tries to spend a lot of time trying answer that question for its personnel by having an extensive orientation program that explains Federal Express's values.

Smith emphasizes that the second question that needs to be answered is, What is in it for me? (Trunick 1989, 19). Federal Express provides tangible evidence of what is in it for employees. It strictly adheres to a policy of promotion from within a career progression. There is an extensive job posting system that keeps employees informed of opportunities. When a position is open, notices are posted throughout the company for all employees to see. Only when no qualified applicants are found inside the company does it begin its search on the outside. Thus there is ample opportunity for all employees to advance within the company. One popular career advancement tool it uses is a tuition refund program, in which it pays tuition of those employed. As would be expected, it employs a lot of students in its main hub and other locations.

INCENTIVES

Career advancement is not the only incentive it uses to increase the odds of being able to retain people. One thing it uses that works well is an awards program. It is designed to reinforce desired behavior, such as quality work and a focus on the customer. Federal Express also believes its incentive program helps it deliver high-quality service and keeps its people motivated.

Acknowledging efforts is essential for a motivated and satisfied work force. In turn, Federal Express knows this acknowledgment stimulates new ideas and encourages better performance and team spirit.

One example of incentive is its Bravo Zulu Voucher Program. It recognizes employees' performances that go above and beyond their normal job responsibilities. Recognition for these acts can range from nonfinancial Bravo Zulu letters of appreciation to cash or noncash awards presented by management personnel.

Another incentive is called Suggestion Awards Program, which encourages employees to submit ideas that will improve operations of the company. These ideas must lower cost, increase productivity, increase revenues, or promote safer working conditions.

Since many companies have suggestion programs, why does this one work? For one thing, it is not simply the handshake and certificate that so often typify suggestion programs. Employees at Federal Express can early $100 to $25,000 for ideas that are implemented. Nice handshake!

One of the nice things about Federal Express's incentives is that the customer is not left out of this reward process. Customers have a voice in selecting outstanding service. The Golden Falcon Award is given to permanent employees who have demonstrated service to their customers that goes above and beyond the call of duty. Candidates for these awards are usually nominated based on unsolicited internal, as well as external, customers' letters citing outstanding performance. Winners of these awards are announced monthly, usually through company publications and video programs. Winners receive an award and, most importantly, shares of stock.

Federal Express's highest award is called the Five Star Award, which is given to individuals for outstanding performance that has materially helped the corporation enhance service, profitability, and teamwork. Several categories of people are eligible for the award, including nonmanagerial employees, managers or senior managers, and managing directors and officers.

COMMUNICATION

Federal Express's success with employee relations and retention depends on candid communication. Smith mentioned that the third question management needs to answer is Where do I go to resolve a problem? (Trunick 1989, 19). He emphasized that Federal Express spends enormous time on its internal employee response program.

The heart of this program is an open-door procedure where employees are encouraged to find answers to situations they find disagreeable, controversial, and/or contrary to existing policy. This open-door policy has no time limit for employees, but it does for management. If an employee expresses concern, management must respond in 14 days. Additionally, Smith and CEO James Barksdale receive a printout of every open-door concern submitted and how and when it was answered.

Questions employees bring up are sent to experts, who can range from a staff person to the CEO. In all cases the person answering the question has a maximum of 14 days to respond. This program focuses on responsiveness, the other plus is its visibility. The CEO not only responds to questions received but also reviews every one of the questions the company receives every week. Direct involvement by upper management makes for an effective tool.

Open doors, especially the way Federal Express uses them, can be effective, but perhaps its most successful communication tool is its renowned Guaranteed Fair Treatment Procedure (GFTP), which it believes is the cornerstone of its people's philosophy. It makes sure any Federal Express employee has the right to have any eligible issue go through a systematic review by progressively higher levels of management. GFTP helps ensure that personnel have a right to discuss complaints with management without fear of retaliation. The company also believes it helps them to maintain an open atmosphere as well as keep its complaint-handling process fair and equitable.

HOW DOES GFTP WORK?

Any person who is disciplined has access to GFTP. It has also been used to resolve other problems or concerns, such as issues involving selection, application of compensation and benefits policies, performance deficiencies, and unacceptable conduct. GFTP is not used to change employment hours, compensation rates, content of benefit policies, or content of corporate personnel policies and procedures. These concerns are addressed through other means, like the open-door policy and suggestion program; the Survey/Feedback/Action policy, which we will look at in a moment, also serves this purpose.

GFTP consists of three basic steps. The first step is referred to as management review and involves employees' submitting a written complaint to a member of management within seven days of an occurrence of an eligible issue. This manager, senior manager, or managing director then reviews all the relevant information. After this person has a grasp of the facts, he or she makes a decision, holds a telephone conference or individual meeting with the complainant, and at that time either upholds, modifies, or overturns the initial management action that was the source of the complaint.

This management review will let the complainant and personnel office know, in writing, about the decision. Federal Express points out that when multiple levels of management are involved in the decision, then a consensus will be reached. This initial part of the review process must occur within ten calendar days of receipt of the complaint unless a written notice of time extension is provided to personnel.

The second step (if necessary) is called the officer review. Officers at Federal Express are a higher rank than managers and are either vice presidents or senior vice presidents of a division. If the complainant is not satisfied with the decision at the end of step one, then he or she can submit a written complaint for officer review. This step must be taken within seven days after step one.

At this stage of GFTP, the vice president or senior vice president reviews all relevant information, conducts an additional investigation, if necessary, and makes a decision to uphold, modify, or overturn earlier management actions. He or she can also initiate a board of review (see last step). Any decision is put in writing and sent to the person complaining. A copy of the written response is also sent to personnel and the complainant's manager. Again, this process must occur within ten days of receipt of the complaint.

APPEALS BOARD

The last step involves an executive review, which follows the same general pattern as the first two steps. The person complaining has seven days after completing step two to submit the complaint to the Employee Relations Department. This department then investigates it and prepares a GFTP case file for the Appeals Board to review.

The Appeals Board again reviews all relevant information and makes a decision to uphold, overturn, initiate a board of review, or take other appropriate actions. All of this must occur within 14 calendar days of receipt of the complaint. The only exception is if a written notice of time extension needed has been sent to both complainant and personnel.

Once a decision has been made, the Appeals Board has three days to respond in writing to the complainant, with a copy going to personnel. This Appeals Board can adjust lower-level decisions, including imposition of more severe discipline. The decision of this Appeals Board is final and binding on the complainant and the company.

As one might imagine, such a complaint process is thorough, but it could be very time-consuming. It takes good organization and streamlining to keep the time reasonable. At Federal Express prior to fiscal year 1986, the average GFTP heard by an Appeals Board (the last step) took 75 days. In fiscal years 1986 and 1987 it took 60 days, and in fiscal year 1988 it took 56 days. For this reason on May 17, 1989, the company changed GFTP to its current process, which was just described.

To speed up the process, Federal Express emphasized that if one is involved in a GFTP, then schedule the meeting as soon as possible. If additional time is required to investigate the facts, then make sure you have enough time to acquire information in a timely manner. Further to ensure speed, communicate your expectations to everyone in your chain and make sure each GFTP file contains all relevant documentation. The purpose is to make sure no time is wasted acquiring these documents.

SURVEY/FEEDBACK/ACTION (SFA)

Federal Express's SFA program complements its GFTP and its other communication tools. SFA is an annual survey of employee attitudes. Each year the survey is used to measure employee opinions and make changes that hopefully enhance those attitudes. Management uses the survey to learn what it needs to improve in specific departments and in the company in general. To ensure that it is a fair gauge of attitudes, it makes sure it is anonymous.

For the last 13 years, Federal Express reported the results of the survey for every group or work unit within the organization. Management never sees individual surveys or responses. Federal Express management requires all managers to meet and discuss employee concerns within six weeks after the work group results have been tallied. If a manager's feedback scores are low, then he or she is expected to develop and implement corrective action.

Action is the key to the company's success with the program. It believes that if people feel they have some real influence, then they are likely to use it. An example of how Federal Express shows that its opinion counts was recounted by its CEO. Fred Smith said that local part-timers were bidding on local full-time jobs, but employees with more seniority and from outside the local area were bumping them and cutting off the part-timers' opportunity to advance. To help solve the problem, Federal Express set up a program where local part-timers receive credit for local service. It hopes this approach will help solve this problem and help keep highly valued employees.

EMPLOYEE TRAINING PROGRAM

Employee retention and relations depend as much on development of employees as on communication and incentives. Corning believes in training. David Luther, senior vice president of quality, says the company expects all employees from forklift operators to division managers to spend 5 percent of their working hours learning new skills (Fierman 1991). The company has also assigned 400 people to train others in their department. It focuses on training, in part, because of an emphasis on team management and a pay-for-knowledge program.

At Corning's Erwin plant in New York, 70 employees (most of whom never went to college) work in teams. Everyone on the four production teams is cross-trained and knows how to operate as well as repair machines, load the kilns, pack and ship, order parts, and control quality.

At Corning, the varied tasks a team member can perform are broken down into four levels of difficulty. Progressing through each level can bring one up to a $2.25-an-hour raise (Fierman 1991). Corning's focus on specific product/process training is impressive, but for sheer size of one's training effort it is hard to surpass Motorola's efforts.

The giant electronics company spends about $60 million a year training its 104,000 employees worldwide. Earlier in the 1980s much of its training money was spent on remedial education so its largely illiterate production work force could master seventh-grade reading and math. Today, employees are trained to do several tasks so they can handle more jobs, work faster, and make fewer mistakes. What has the company gained out of all this training? Motorola says it has saved over $1.5 billion in three years, mostly because of the improvements the training has made in its work force (Fierman 1991). In some operations, Motorola gets $33 out of every dollar spent in training.

On the average, Motorola provides 1 million hours of training per year for its employees. In 1987 its spending on training represented 2.4 percent of the corporate payroll. Of that amount today, about 40 percent goes to quality improvement processes, principles, technology, and objectives (Smith). In addition to developing training programs, it also makes use of "course maps," which help employees and their managers select programs that meet an individual's needs.

Training consists of three parts. The first is Motorola Training and Education Center (MTEC), which provides training at all levels with special emphasis on providing all employees with the knowledge and skills to achieve corporate goals. The other two types of training include product/process specific training and special management training.

MTEC's main focus is on quality-related training since Motorola is recognized as a quality leader. These programs include training in statistical process control, design for manufacturability, and helping employees understand how the company plans a 100-fold improvement in its process. Courses provide employees with problem-solving strategies and tools so they can help achieve this goal. MTEC is also used as a framework around which more specific product/process training occurs.

Part of its training efforts also involves its Motorola Management Institute (MMI), an intensive two-week program on design, manufacturing, and quality issues intended for manufacturing, design, and operational managers at senior and support positions. To object is to enhance leadership and decision-making skills. MMI subjects also include customer-centered culture and marketing for world-class manufacturing and quality, designing for manufacturability, cycle time management, and how to implement change. Leading experts are brought in to present the latest information.

Like Motorola and Corning, Federal Express retains employees, as well as improves their skills, by making sure its employees receive proper training in job performance skills. To help improve its training, Federal Express in 1986 implemented an Interactive Video Instruction (IVI).

IVI is used for new information training and test preparation. (Customer service employees are tested twice a year on job knowledge.) A big advantage of the IVI program is that it allows employees to take advantage of slack periods to train themselves at any time. Employees can proceed at their own pace, and training can be repeated as much as necessary. According to Federal Express, IVI helps standardize information and reduce training time by 60 percent. IVI is even used for new hire orientation.

Other training for nonmanagers used by Federal Express includes its Leadership Evaluation and Awareness Program (LEAP), which qualifies non-management employees for management positions. The process requires employees to fill out a leadership questionnaire that measures nine characteristics of a leader. There are a formal critique from employees and managers, a written exam, panel interview, oral presentation, and peer assessment.

Managers are not left out of this training process. Federal Express uses a three-day in-depth program called Management Applied Personnel Skills (MAPS) training program. It is designed to provide background information an hands-on application on a variety of personnel and legal issues normally encountered in the workplace. A minimum of five classes are offered monthly, with one in each of the regions of the company and one in the home office at Memphis, Tennessee.

In addition to MAPS, Federal Express has a Leadership Institute, which is a full week of required management training for all new managers. The institute also teaches quality management, leadership concepts, and company philosophy.

CONCLUDING THOUGHTS

Smith believes it is important for people to take pride in what they do. In Federal Express's case he points out the importance of the cargo it carries. It is essential for managers to make sure employees know what they should do and why it is important. There must be some ulterior reason, some higher-level purpose for work rather than just earning a paycheck. They need a sense of purpose and rewards for a job well done. Equally important, they must have the power to influence what is done and how it is done.

Federal Express's, Motorola's, and Corning's formulas for retaining employees are good ones, but certainly not the only ones. They may not be appropriate for your organization, but one point is universal: if we hope to keep our employees, then we must think more comprehensively how those people will fit in and how we keep them involved so they do not want to leave. In the following chapters, we will look at other techniques and tools for improving retention and relations.

NOTE

Part of this chapter previously appeared in SAM Journal. Used with permission.

REFERENCES

Fierman, Jaclyn. "Shaking the Blue-Collar Blues." *Fortune*, April 22, 1991, 216–17.

Smith, Bill. *The Motorola Story* (in-house publication).

Trunick, Perry A. "Leadership and People Distinguish Federal Express." *Transportation and Distribution*, December 1989, 19.

6

Delayered, Downsized, and Demotivated

Federal Express's low turnover rate and ability to retain employees are certainly impressive. However, even the best-run companies are going to find it increasingly difficult to keep their best employees. Even when a company has respect for its people, it may not be enough to keep the best and brightest of them.

Federal Express is seen as a good place to work not only because of its good employee relations but also because of the opportunity to succeed. It is a company still on the growth curve as it seeks to become a global competitor. If one has the ability and desire, there are still chances to get ahead.

A lot of things seem better when there are opportunities for advancement, but what if you work in a company where those opportunities are extremely remote? Increasingly, that situation is just what seems to be happening. While there are opportunities for employment, there are not nearly as many for advancement.

WHAT PROMOTIONS?

Every time you turn around today, someone seems to be talking about the flattening of organizations. This delayering of organizational levels has primarily focused on eliminating middle managers and first-line supervisors. *Business Week* reports that nationwide since 1960, U.S. companies have eliminated nearly one of every four middle management positions (Weber, Driscoll, and Brandt 1990).

People talk of empowering employees, but what does all that mean when there is no longer an "up"? Where do you go? How do you motivate people? How do you keep people if there are few promotions and chances to move up? Ross A. Webber, management professor at the University of Pennsylvania's Wharton School of Business, says that in the 1960s and early 1970s fast trackers were being promoted every 18 to 24 months. Now he says this time has at least doubled (Weber, Driscoll, and Brandt 1990). In many cases, pay has not kept pace with those levels a few years ago.

The demographic bulge of some 81 million baby boomers is in the middle of our corporations. Just as this expanded group of workers moves through middle management, companies are restricting middle management positions. The result is fewer rungs on the ladder. Surveys have shown a growing managerial dissatisfaction with both what these managers have attained and the responsibilities they have acquired. Furthermore, talks of recession and wars and uncertainty only further strengthen the desire of companies to remain lean and mean.

ALTERNATIVES

When the rules change and promotions and upward movement are unlikely, then it is time to rethink our traditional motivators. We need innovative approaches like those used by Chicago's Hyatt Corporation. At Hyatt, the promotions, like those in many corporations, do not come frequently. Many young managers going into hotel management will wait longer before getting a chance to run a hotel. One of Hyatt's solutions, which we will examine in greater detail in the last chapter, was to help some if its managers start a new business.

Hyatt tells the story of John Allegretti, who, at 23, was an assistant housekeeping manager. He was ready to quit his job because of the repetition. He was looking for something different, something a little more challenging. One of Hyatt's vice presidents, Don DePorter, did not want to lose Allegretti, so he put him in charge of a project he was interested in, namely, reducing waste at some of the Hyatt hotels. The project turned out to be so successful that management let him develop and run a new waste consulting company for Hyatt. Besides Hyatt, the recycle company now has 24 clients in eight states (Weber, Driscoll, and Brandt 1990). Hyatt not only has a new and successful venture but also has a very involved and satisfied employee (Ellis 1990).

The experience with John Allegretti was not Hyatt's only experience with innovative approaches that are good for business and motivation. In the last chapter we shall see how Hyatt, along with other companies, is helping its employees take novel ideas occurring outside their core business and convert them into free-standing companies.

RESTRUCTURING

There are many innovative alternatives to empowering and motivating people, many of which we will look at in the last chapter. Sometimes, though, the best approach may be to simplify work. As it is unrealistic to expect to set everyone up in his or her own business, what can be done? There are many simple, but effective, alternatives. In addition to setting up new business ventures, Hyatt does simple things like conduct monthly sessions with its workers where employees discuss issues that are bothering them. (More about these types of approaches when we discuss Face-to-Face communications in a later chapter.) These same workers are given a chance to critique anonymously and then discuss the quality of their boss's leadership. While such simple communication tools help diffuse discontent, permanent improvements in the workplace depend on restructuring work.

One way to do this restructuring of work involves broadening job responsibilities. For instance, General Electric (G.E.) went through a process of reducing the number of managerial layers within its organization, in some cases, from four to two levels. To improve motivation and allow more lateral movement within the organization, G.E. reduced pay grades so managers in different disciplines could move easily across the organization. It also broadened the responsibilities of many of the managerial positions. The hope was that broader responsibilities would increase the challenge and satisfaction with "flatter" organizations. PepsiCo, TRW, and others are currently going through similar broadening experiments in the hope of increasing motivation and satisfaction.

DuPont tries to give its managers more autonomy and freedom within jobs. Years ago if someone had an idea to try something different, there were the normal frustration and administrative hassles associated with introducing new ideas in large bureaucratic organizations. Things are starting to change. Kurt M. Landgraf of DuPont gave an example of how things are changing when he said that his request for $5 million for a new generic drug venture needed approval of only one manager above him (Weber, Driscoll, and Brandt 1990).

This broadening of managerial responsibilities seems to be a trend. At PepsiCo's Taco Bell, the benefits plan manager can also now get involved in recruiting. TRW engineers receive broad research budgets and broad latitude to work on projects. DuPont, TRW, and most other organizations have not, however, broadened the responsibilities and autonomy of most of their managers; after all, there are risks to giving people more freedom and control, and they are likely to fare poorly if they are not properly prepared and educated on how to handle increased responsibility. Increasingly, it is clear that if we hope to keep today's aggressive and upwardly mobile managers motivated in a nonmobile organizations, then we have to rethink how we expect managers to function.

SIMPLIFY

One of the things that we must rethink is the content of most jobs. For many, the main frustration of a job is not the lack of mobility, but rather the sheer frustration of trying to do their job. Many jobs contain more "busy" work and less productive work. How many times do you feel your main function is filling out reams and reams of paperwork, reading one useless report after another, and being asked to do one irrelevant task after another? It seems someone is always looking over your shoulder to make sure every *i* is dotted and every *t* is crossed.

If you think about it, you fill out much of that paperwork because someone does not trust your judgment. It seems every time you must get approval, someone is saying you do not have enough knowledge or ability to make the decision yourself.

Obviously, this view is particularly pessimistic. In fact, some double-checking is necessary, but American organizations have been severely criticized for running bloated organizations with far too much double-checking and inspecting, too much indirect labor, and not enough direct labor.

Typical of this situation was a DuPont case in which a research and development (R&D) unit had 16 research managers manage its R&D efforts. As a result, a lot of time was taken up with paperwork, filing, and the normal administrative activities. Now, this same unit has only two research managers, who have a lot less paperwork and get more work done. In the next chapter, we will look at how companies like G.E. are able to get the work out through eliminating, simplifying, and combining work.

LATERAL MOVES

Where do you move when you cannot move up? PepsiCo has been one of the leaders at encouraging lateral moves across divisions as a means of motivating its people. For some it does take a different mind-set even to accept lateral moves. Initially, it may be difficult for hard chargers to accept what many consider to be the slow track, but things are changing.

At one time a brief tenure in a job, as one moved up through the organization, was fairly typical. A slow track was seen as a career death sentence. Certainly things have changed for some of the more competitive companies. At PepsiCo, now it is standard practice for every six of ten management-track staffers to take this slow track (Weber, Driscoll, and Brandt 1990). Executives bounce from Kentucky Fried Chicken to Frito-Lay to overseas on a regular basis. More and more today, lateral moves, or a zigzag career, is not only OK, but the preferred way to the top.

The old way of business, with brief tenures in jobs as one moved up through the organization, had its downside. For one thing, people had limited knowledge about any area. For another, it tended to focus everyone on the short term. In today's highly competitive environment, limited knowledge of how the corporation works as a whole is a luxury few can afford.

Frequently in the past, managers advanced up the organization through narrow careers paths, sometimes moving far up a marketing ladder before getting some general managerial experience. As a result, they had limited ability because they spent their entire time in one career. Japanese companies, by contrast, have given younger managers broad experience first. The result is they end up with more knowledgeable managers. Many American companies are now beginning to follow suit. At DuPont, engineers often spend an initial six-year period working in different areas before coming to rest in one department.

Zigzagging can also occur through overseas' assignments. Companies today often find it necessary to compete in today's global marketplace. Sometimes these managers receive no new title; sometimes they do get something highly prized by today's companies, namely, diversity of experience. When you consider that it is not uncommon for companies like DuPont to do nearly half their sales in foreign markets, it is easy to see why companies see foreign service as a real plus.

Overseas is not the only foreign experience that companies are finding to be both motivational as well as beneficial to the company. Many are sending their most promising executives back to school. DuPont sent some of its managers on academic sabbatical. Personnel like Phillis K. Allen, a molecular biologist from DuPont, found the experience renewing (Weber, Driscoll, and Brandt 1990). She was very impressed, as anyone would be, with DuPont's $30,000 investment to send her to the Sloan School of Management for her formal education in general management skills.

DuPont and others are trying to use lateral moves as a motivational tool. While pay, managerial level, and, in some cases, even titles remain the same, the challenge of each new job keeps many hard chargers, and no-so-hard chargers, motivated. Clearly, zigzagging can be good for people, as well as for the corporation—if people can grow through the experience.

This broadening and restructuring jobs can be a partial answer to motivating today's work force. It, along with creating new business ventures, is not the total answer. For some, zigzagging will always be perceived as too slow, even when they know the experience is beneficial. On the other hand, some personality types may be even more well suited for today's zigzagging. Chances are they will be the ones who are not so concerned about a title as they are for a chance to broaden their knowledge and ability. Zigzagging should appeal to those who seek a better balance between family and work. It should appeal to those who like more flexibility and choice.

Not too long ago if you turned down a promotion or move, that pretty well ended your career. Today that does not have to be the case. If you turn down lateral movies, if you turn down opportunities, there will still be a chance for other opportunities. Delaying those moves gives both the manager and corporation more time to evaluate and assess.

ASSOCIATES

Wal-Mart was one of the first to use the term *associates*, but others will surely follow and it will undoubtedly be used more and more frequently. In some cases, when upper management uses the term, it is mostly symbolic. In other cases, it indicates significant changes that are occurring within organizations. Why the talk about "associates" rather than "employees"? The simple answer is that many managers believe it is easier to motivate associates rather than employees.

At Gore and Associates, each of its 5,300 employees is an associate. There are no bosses, only team leaders who are responsible for leading and motivating. At Gore, every associate has someone who is their mentor and counselor.

Associates at Gore meet every six months to rank peers by assessing their contribution to the group. Committees are then used to merge these lists and set raises, ranking pay from the highest to the lowest (Weber 1990). Leaders at Gore cannot give orders, only seek commitments from associates.

While all of equality is impressive, it is the culture that seems most motivational. Anyone can and does take ideas or complaints to anyone else. When Robert Gore, the founder, saw that some 200 staffers were seen as more important than others he opened the meeting to a broader cross section of staffers. No trouble with motivated people here.

POWER OF CULTURE

Compaq Computer Corporation was formed in 1982. In 1983, it was recognized as the fastest growing company in U.S. history. It did the same in 1984 and became the most successful second-year company in U.S. history. By 1985, it became the first company to reach the Fortune 500 in less than four years. In 1987, it passed $1 billion in sales; in 1988,

$2 billion; now, over $3 billion (Webber 1990). The heart of its success, says its CEO, is its culture.

Ron Canion, CEO and president of Compaq, says, "If you spend 80 percent or 90 percent or, if you're really lucky, 98 percent or 99 percent of your time on productive things, you leave work feeling you've accomplished things" (Weber 1990, 116). To keep its feeling of productivity and community, Compaq holds quarterly meetings with the entire company. Usually four meetings are held over a two-day period. In these meetings, it goes over performance, shows videos, and talks about a wide range of issues from simple to complex. The important point is to build a sense of purpose and community.

Canion says you cannot have continuity unless you keep your turnover low, as Compaq does. He says most companies talk of compensation, stock options, and bonuses in an effort to retain their people but many are missing the mark. He believes it is more a matter of whether people feel drained or emotionally charged. People stay when they enjoy what they do. They stay when they enjoy work. He says that people stay when they fit the culture and when they are working in a supportive, helpful environment and get fulfillment from working as part of a winning organization (Webber 1990).

CONSENSUS AS A MOTIVATIONAL TOOL

Compaq makes extensive use of consensus decision making. This does not mean that everyone has to agree, only that people believe that the right facts and right reasons are used to make the right decision (Webber 1990). Canion believes the real benefit of the consensus process is not that you get an answer but that you go through the process to get the answer.

Consensus decision making makes your people think about the decision, and you get commitment and motivation from the process. Later, we will look at how Compaq and others are using consensus management even at the lowest level to motivate people. It is called "team management."

Good teams keep pushing and keep digging for facts until everyone agrees on a decision. The objective is to get the facts and get the best answer. Working as a true team also involves using a democratic approach. At Compaq how an idea or suggestion is handled makes it effective.

Sometimes when a team evaluates an idea, it is up to the boss to look at the choices, then make the decision. Compaq does not assume just because someone is the boss, he or she has the final answer. The boss contributes early in the decision process rather than at the end. Teams at Compaq do not get the boss's approval, only input. Compaq clearly shows that testing ideas and getting people thinking, asking questions, testing assumptions, and listening are all tools to lower turnover and raise involvement.

CONCLUDING THOUGHTS

Keeping people motivated and happy has always been a challenge, but it seems much more so today. There are motivational problems as companies becomes leaner, more competitive. The lack of promotion due to flatter organization makes it harder to keep people motivated. When there are fewer rungs on the ladder and less room in the middle, how do you keep employees motivated, or simply just keep them?

Ron Canion, DEO for Compaq, seems to have said it best. He says people "stay when they enjoy what they do." They stay when they fit in with the culture. Many suggestions have been given to make work more enjoyable, and many more will be suggested. Reducing managerial layers so it is easier to communicate and get things done, increasing autonomy, broadening responsibilities, and simplifying work are all potential ways to make work more enjoyable. There is no option—we must retain our best and improve relations with all employees to remain competitive. We need to restructure work so it is more enjoyable.

REFERENCES

Ellis, James E. "Feeling Stuck at Hyatt? Create a New Business." *Business Week*, December 10, 1990, 195.

Webber, Alan M. "Consensus, Continuity, and Common Sense." *Harvard Business Review* 68 (July–August 1990): 116.

Weber, Joseph. "No Bosses and Even 'Leaders' Can't Give Orders." *Business Week*, December 10, 1990, 196–97.

Weber, Joseph, Lisa Driscoll, and Richard Brandt. "Farewell, Fast Track." *Business Week*, December 10, 1990, 192–96.

7

Job Redesign

Finding and keeping employees are difficult but not enough; the real trick is to keep them productive and happy, a result especially difficult in times of downsizing, labor shortages, and restructuring. The size of this problem was seen by the Society for Human Resource Management, which surveyed 1,468 restructured companies. It found that productivity either stayed the same or deteriorated after the layoffs (Henkoff 1990). An out-placement firm, the Right Associates, said 70 percent of senior managers at recently downsized companies said their workers had low morale, feared future cutbacks, and distrusted management (Henkoff 1990).

Clearly, it is not enough just to keep people from leaving, nor is it wise simply to eliminate them. There are no automatic improvements. Either way you lose. It takes planning and restructuring of work itself for employees to stay and remain productive.

Most human resource managers and others want employees to assume more responsibility and take risks, but be accountable. They want the quality of work to improve, and they want to keep the customer in mind. Companies need speed and better decisions. As the old saying goes, Work smarter, not harder.

What money managers fail to recognize is that employees, as well as managers, want the same thing. People leave companies or lose interest in the job because of the enormous frustrations of trying to do a job that is not logical. People of average intelligence get frustrated when they believe the company or higher-level officials put so many roadblocks in their path that it simply becomes too hard to fight the good fight. It is the year-after-year tackling of immovable objects, of dealing with asinine rules and procedures, that leads to stress and burnout—but it does not have to be that way.

ELIMINATE, SIMPLIFY, AND COMBINE

The phrase "Eliminate, simplify, and combine" is an old engineering term that is often associated with job design. It represents an attitude, rather than any specific technique. The attitude is one of constantly challenging every task, every step within a task to see if there is a better way. You are always trying to find ways of eliminating any work or part of the work. If parts of the work cannot be eliminated, then maybe some aspects of the job can be simplified or combined.

For instance, if you cannot *eliminate* a move or inspect it, maybe you can at least *simplify* it, by using a gauge to check something. If you cannot eliminate an inspection or other step then maybe at least it can be *combined* with some other activity, say, the work itself. Therefore, operators can inspect their own work rather than doing the work and then having someone inspect it for them. The goal of such thinking is not to get people to work faster; rather it is to make work easier to do. You cannot make people work faster (at least over the long haul), but you can make work easier. If it is easier, more people will enjoy it, and if it is enjoyable, then the speed will take care of itself.

There is another reason for making work easier, beyond the speed or productivity that will occur. If you make work easier by eliminating, simplifying, or combining steps, tasks, or jobs, then people will be less stressed, less frustrated. They will tend to stay longer, and that result affects the bottom line.

One such example involved Oryx, a Dallas Texas–based oil and gas producer, which saved $70 million in operating cost in one year by simply eliminating rules, procedures, reviews, reports, and approvals that had little to do with the business (Henkoff 1990).

The company was able to reap these profits by setting up teams that took a fresh look at its operation. As a result of this internal audit, it was able to eliminate 25 percent of all internal reports and reduced the number of signatures needed for capital expenditures from 20 to 4 (Henkoff 1990). Before this audit, it took seven months to produce an annual budget; now it takes only six weeks.

Such inefficiencies in day-to-day operation are far from uncommon. Most companies have enormous extra or irrelevant work built into their process, but to eliminate, simplify, or combine, you first have to know what you do. That alone may tell you what you need to do to improve things.

Colgate-Palmolive Company provides us with an example of these potential savings. It devised a questionnaire for its "technical group managers" to find out how they were spending their time. It found that its scientists were spending far too much of their time on supervising and reporting rather than on making teeth whiter and clothes brighter.

ELIMINATING WORK

Irrelevant work is a common problem that can be eliminated. Unnecessary work can involve procedures, rules, regulations, and even corporate rituals. Even the most basic task can have inefficiencies that have become standard operational procedures. Consider the case of Maids International, a $16 million a year housecleaning service that hires part-time employees, mostly women, for $4.25 to $7.50 an hour (Stewart 1990).

Its labor is drawn from the same pool that applies to fast food, hotel, and other entry-level businesses. Management felt the company could not afford the high turnover that is characteristic of those businesses, so it looked at the way its work was organized. The company found problems that were adversely affecting its employees, but, contrary to what you might think, excessive, irrelevant reports or their approval process was not the problem. What it discovered was that the actual physical work needed to be redesigned. CEO Dan Bishop said, "Fatigue and boredom are what burn people out. We tried to eliminate them" (Stewart 1990, 124).

The company tried to eliminate physical fatigue and boredom by focusing on each employee's job. It broke down jobs to look at each step and discovered several commonsense changes that could be made to reduce employee fatigue and boredom. It knew that simple improvements add up when they are done thousands of time. Now, employees wind a vacuum cord in three seconds versus the eight it used to take. After its simple methods improvement, employees bend only 30 times while cleaning an average house, compared with the 72 it used to take before the analysis of work methods (Stewart 1990). Other improvements that reduced boredom included rotating jobs so that the person who cleans a kitchen at one location will clean the living room at another. One result of this method analysis is that now entry-level employees stay an average of nine months as opposed to the five months or less that entry-level employees stay at McDonald's. Since Maids International essentially uses the same labor pool as McDonald's, that reduction is an important competitive advantage.

Pizza Hut is another service that is investing time redesigning its jobs. Results of its redesign had a positive effect on employees. For instance, morale increased when store managers helped decide what corporate paperwork could be eliminated. The point is, anyone can do method

Figure 7.1
Step-By-Step Process for Eliminating, Simplifying, and Combining

Step 1	Observe and understand current decision-making process.
Step 2	Document decisions by using a flow chart. (This would involve writing a detailed description of the decision-making process to be studied, listing every individual decision [or non-decision] that is made as well as how one gets from one decision point to the next.)
Step 3	The key is to critically evaluate each step of the current decision-making process and any proposed changes in it. (This is where creativity and persistence pays off. Consider layout, organizational structure, and training, among other options, as ways of eliminating, simplifying or combining steps.)
Step 4	Implement the change. (Ideas are important, but they will not help until they are implemented. Someone has to have patience and persistence to specify what is to be done, to assign responsibilities, and to follow up to see that instructions have been carried out.
Step 5	After sufficient time has passed, revise the decision-making steps when and as necessary.

analysis; you do not have to be an engineer. Most of the improvements are common sense.

While suggested improvements, like those of Pizza Hut and Maids International, may be commonsense management, they are not always seen easily. First, they require the right attitude toward a job and second, a specific problem-solving approach. Those who are most likely to find improvements are those who are always asking, "Why?" They are always curious why something has to be done a certain way. Such an attitude is needed if you are to challenge each job and each step within a job. You should ask what is involved, where and when it occurs, who does it, and how it occurs. Ask yourself why the job or any step in the job needs to be done. Try to think of ways of eliminating each step or a part of each step. If you cannot eliminate it, then maybe you can at least simplify it or combine it with another step, so the job or step is easier to do. The main point is to follow a step-by-step, rational process of analyzing a job. A summary of this process is seen in Figure 7.1.

There are numerous aids for people wishing to perfect their skills at improving work methods. You could audit a motion and methods class at a local college, or you can read numerous books on the subject, several of which are provided at the end of this chapter.

CHALLENGING ASSUMPTIONS

While the process of analyzing job steps and methods is straightforward (get rid of wasteful and unnecessary tasks), the analysis may lead to some surprises. Never go into the analysis with any assumptions. It is what the management at Heinz calls "paradigm busting." *Fortune* magazine reported that Heinz's Ore-Ida factory in Plover, Wisconsin (Henkoff 1990), was having trouble with its French fries, which were being rejected. It examined every step along the way, starting when the spuds were first unloaded at the factory. Engineers at the Ore-Ida factory had assume that uncooked spuds were tough enough to withstand 3- to 14-foot drops as they moved through their production process—that assumption was their paradigm. The spuds were not breaking outright, but they were developing microscopic fault lines that led to fractures father down the line (Henkoff 1990). The company installed a few metal slides and saved $300,000.

As the old adage goes, never assume. For instance, never assume you need to eliminate people to improve performance. Sometimes it might be better to add them. Heinz found, at least in one case, that when it added employees and slowed down its production line, its cost-effectiveness went up; it was able to save $250 by midyear! Here is how it happened.

In earlier times Heinz-Starkist tuna-canning factories in Puerto Rico and American Samoa had cut their work force by 5 percent in response to tough competition; specifically, they feared low-wage rivals in Thailand. Management's concern was more on productivity than on quality. As a consequence, the factories were losing tons of meat on the bone every workday. They solved the problem by hiring 400 new hourly employees and five new supervisors and installing four new lines to take the load off the current lines. In the end the changes meant an increase of $5 million in labor cost but saved $15 million in wastage; and thus saved $10 million.

WORK OUT

One of the most famous and large-scale cases of redesigning work involves one of America's largest corporations, General Electric (G.E.), a highly diversified corporation ranging from NBC television to G.E. plastics and aircraft engines. G.E. has been around for over 100 years, with a market value of over $58 billion. It employs 300,000 people, but unfortunately those are not its only big figures.

Diversity and size alone make the corporation susceptible to bureaucracy. This is where its CEO, Jack Welch, comes in. Under the previous CEO, G.E. went from cash shortages to a position of financial strength. Along the way a huge bureaucracy was created resembling a military command structure. Enter Welch, a former engineer, who regards "bureaucracy as evil" because it destroys productivity by distracting attention from useful work. He believes it makes people look inward, at the organization, rather than outward, to the customer and the competition (Sherman 1989)

An outcome of this attitude is a program called "Work Out," which is G.E.'s systematic attempt to eliminate unnecessary work by eliminating unnecessary meetings, reports, approvals, and tasks. The process starts with regularly scheduled "town meetings" designed to bring together large sections of the business to discuss ways of eliminating work. People from manufacturing, engineering, and customer service are involved. The suggestions of salaried, as well as lower-level and entry-level, people are solicited.

The purpose of these meetings is straightforward—eliminate bureaucracy, including multiple approvals, unnecessary paperwork, excessive reports, and even corporate rituals that prove ineffective. One such town meeting occurred in G.E.'s medical systems business X-ray unit near Milwaukee. The unit came up with 55 items that could be eliminated or improved. In one case a group determined that the head of its computer lab should be allowed to spend petty cash and sign for deliveries (Sherman 1989).

In a classic case of overmanagement, G.E. used to employ 1,000 people who worked nights and weekends, at the end of each quarter, just so G.E. could be the first company of its size to report earnings publicly. What it discovered, through its Work Out efforts, was that, in the words of Welch, "Who the heck cares?" Maybe at one time someone did, but not now. This reexamining process is enabling G.E. to eliminate, simplify, and combine and in the process become leaner and more competitive.

The important point is that G.E.'s Work Out process is not an isolated effort but is an integral part of its philosophy of streamlining the company and trying to bring it into the twenty-first century. Programs die and any process takes constant attention and care; otherwise it is just another management fad. To be good at work redesign, a company must have a philosophy of continual improvement and, ultimately, a cultural change.

Another company that provides a shining example of building a redesigned process around a philosophy of continual improvement is Motorola. It is a global competitor and the first winner of the nation's award for highest quality, the Malcolm Baldridge Award, given to those select few with outstanding customer service and quality standards. Much of the company's success is based on a process called Six Sigma.

SIX SIGMA

Bill Wiggenhorn, then vice president and director of Motorola's training and simulation, expressed the philosophy of Six Sigma: "to get the process right the first time—but only do it if it is a value-added step." Six Sigma is a statistical concept that has been operationally defined by Motorola as not having more than 3.4 defects per million opportunities. This standard is considerably higher than the quality standards used by typical companies.

The only way Motorola can achieve this level of quality is to reduce dramatically the product variability that is common due to ineffective product design, lack of process control, and inferior suppliers. It will have to reduce cycle times and increase the level of both product and service quality. A coordinated effort is necessary to reduce variation in everything the company does, including office filing, typing, and so on. Some of the tools used include Statistical Process Control (SPC), preventative maintenance, vendor certification, and standardization and simplification of parts and production.

SIX STEPS OF SIX SIGMA

An example of the coordinated effort needed was described by George Fisher, president and CEO, who explained the six steps necessary to achieve these lofty goals. All persons and departments must first identify the product or service they provide. His comments were in reference to the company's philosophy about customer service and quality improvement. In reference to customers they serve, employees should ask themselves, "What do I do?" The answer could range from manufacturing a tangible product to assessing something being communicated to those outside their group or department. Second, they should identify the customers for their product or service and determine what they consider important. Employees should ask, "For whom do I work?" and, to answer this question, ask each customer, "What product or service do you need from us?" and "Why do you need it?" Sometimes the answer to this question may be obvious; sometimes it is not. Third is a need to identify what the employee needs to satisfy the customer. Each person must ask, "What do I need to do my work better?" This question is the essence of trying to make improvements by eliminating, simplifying, or combining. Information can come from phone calls, physical equipment, or other data. Once people have determined their needs, they can then sit down with those who supply them with goods and services and determine what they need to do their work.

The fourth step is for employees to define the process for doing their work and ask, "How can I specifically define my work?" Defining work means breaking down each operation of a job into steps and tasks and then identifying the detailed inputs and outputs for each step. This process can involve developing a flowchart and diagram of a person's present way of doing work, to see graphically what is involved and can help spot areas prone to error. Once this step is done, key areas can then be measured to see where too little or too much time is being spent.

The next step is the critical design process. In this case, Motorola's objective is to make tasks as mistake-proof as possible and eliminate wasted effort. The central question for anyone wanting to eliminate, simplify, or combine is, "How can I do work better?" The answer might include eliminating or simplifying tasks, increasing training, or changing methodology—if possible, eliminating those steps that do not add value or at least simplifying or combining them with other steps. This change eliminates waste.

The final step in Motorola's process to ensure continuous improvement by measuring, analyzing, and controlling the improvement process. Again a flowchart can be used not only to document changes but also graphically to show the total savings, regardless of whether one uses a flowchart or not. It is important for people continuously to examine how well they are doing their work. Among other things this step may involve tracking and recording the time it takes to do jobs. What is important is to find some way of measuring and evaluating what employees do, not accepting the status quo, always benchmarking the process, and then finding ways of improving efforts. This process of benchmarking and trying to continuously improve is Motorola's secret to improving performance.

CONCLUDING THOUGHTS

Becoming a world-class competitor able to compete with the Japanese or anyone else means continuously analyzing and organizing operations. Instead of separate and disjointed efforts, everyone must focus his or her efforts toward the same direction of eliminating, simplifying, or combining tasks so work is performed more effectively. There must be a clear strategy. In Motorola's case, it first identified how to please the customer. Once these needs were identified, then it determined how it stacked up against the competition. It is important never to accept the current situation. Business should always be in the process of updating its method of measurement, making changes, and improving the production of goods or delivery of service.

Motorola provides a shining example of what can be done. The centerpiece of its philosophy is its Six Sigma quality program (Wiggenhorn 1988). It sets impressive goals, then maps out a way to meet those goals. Its approach consists of having all employees within the organization first identify what product or service they are providing, identifying specifically who their customers are, and then deciding what is needed to do a better job of satisfying them. Once these parameters are isolated, employees define, through flowcharts and other means, the process for doing work. It is then feasible to try to make the process as mistake-proof as possible. In the final analysis, total customer satisfaction and employee satisfaction can occur only if business sets itself on the path of continuously trying to improve the service and products offered by getting to know its customers better.

REFERENCES

Henkoff, Ronald. "Cost Cutting: How to Do It Right." *Fortune*, April 9, 1990, 40–48.

Sherman, Stratford. "Inside the Mind of Jack Welch." *Fortune*, March 27, 1989, 38.

Stewart, Thomas A. "Do You Push Your People Too Hard?" *Fortune*, October 22, 1990, 124.

Wiggenhorn, Bill. "Achieving Six Sigma Quality." *Opportunities* 5, no. 2 (February 1988): 2.

ADDITIONAL READING ON MOTION AND METHODS ANALYSIS

Aft, Lawrence S. *Productivity Measurement and Improvement*. Reston, Virginia: Reston, 1983.

Barnes, Ralph M. *Motion and Time Study Design and Measurement of Work*. New York: John Wiley and Sons, 1968. (Barnes's work is more technical, but not difficult to read, than the rest of the references. Many consider this early work and later editions to be the bible of methods study.)

Gilbert, Owen. *A Manager's Guide to Work Study*. New York: John Wiley and Sons, 1968, 5–32.

Management Problem Analysis. St. Paul, MN: Management Center, College of St. Thomas, 1971.

Methods Improvement for the Supervisor. American Management Association, New York, NY: 1964.

Techniques of Work Simplification. Department of the Army pamphlet, No. 1–52, 1967.

8

Flextime

In today's competitive workplace employers must remain attuned to the needs of their work force. Those who do will have a distinct advantage. One of the tools being used by United States firms to meet this objective is the use of flextime. The reason is simple: it is very popular, from the employee's viewpoint. A recent survey showed that 78 percent of the respondents favored flexible work schedules so they could spend more time with their families, even if the scheduled meant slower career advancement (Baumann 1990).

The concept of flextime refers to a variety of flexible arrangements, including unconventional hours, part-time work, job sharing, leaves of absence, and working at home. From a company's perspective, allowing employees to work fewer and more flexible hours is a powerful way to attract and retain top-caliber people.

From the employees' perspective, flexible work arrangements give them a greater sense of empowerment. Flextime gives many a stronger feeling that their company trusts them. Additionally, in these times of dual-career parents, it helps parents raise their children more responsibly. It also turns out that professionals who have such arrangements are fiercely loyal to their employers (Deutschman 1991).

Consider the cases of two workers. Renee Garbos was a manager of a project at PepsiCo. She asked for an unusual schedule after the birth of her child. The company cooperated, and now she works three ten-hour days a week—Tuesday, Wednesday, and Thursday. As she says, "allowing me to work this way shows the company cares about me" (Deutschman 1991).

Wendy Hoerner, a Steelcase product engineer, wanted to work only on mornings. Reluctantly, the company agreed. She was able to handle her job, and when conspicuously pregnant with her second child, she was promoted to senior product engineer. As she said, "I got a kick out of that—a pregnant part-timer being promoted."

SHARED JOBS

Not all flextime involves working less time or different days. Sometimes employees can share the work. Employees who wish to share often must write a lengthy proposal spelling out, in detail, how sharing will work (Deutschman 1991). For example, how long will it last and what happens if one of the job sharers leaves? Such a document is a good planning tool for anyone wanting to share jobs. The key to making it work is good communication between partners who use phone calls, written updates, electronic mail, and spiral-bound logs to keep up-to-date. Most companies normally pay these work sharers 120 percent of what one person would make in the job. Thus, a sharer gets about three-fifths of a regular salary plus some benefits.

Why go to all the trouble? It comes back to retention and relations. Aetna Life and Casualty's experience is fairly typical. In 1988, 23 percent of the women taking maternity leave did not return. Notes Sherry Herchenroether, director of family services: "They tended to be high performers. That's what really concerned us" (Deutschman 1991, 60). Aetna offered six-month unpaid parental leave and also encouraged managers to offer these employees part-time work when their leave expired. Such a policy is used by such firms as Federal Express, Hewlett-Packard, and Merck.

Not all flextime is creative; sometimes it simply means shifting the time you come in to work. Flextime for Federal Express means some of its employees can arrive ten minutes before the shift begins and leave ten minutes early or arrive ten minutes later and leave ten minutes later than those on a "normal" shift.

Hewlett-Packard was one of the first to start to do away with time clocks. Today the plan, which was started in its German plant, is uniformly adopted throughout the company.

Under HP's plan, there is a window for starting work of about two hours, say from 6:30 A.M. to 8:30 A.M. (Hewlett 1982). During this window employes can start work, put in their eight hours, and then go home. William Hewlett notes that employees love the plan and he is convinced that HP gets better productivity from its people because of the plan. Hewlett-Packard, like others, tries to fit flextime to their own company's needs. For instance, it tried a four-day, ten-hour workday plan, which did not work, so the plan was dropped.

Merck, the giant and highly successful medical organization, has made extensive use of flextime. In the following pages, we will look at the detailed program and how the company implemented it. Information was provided by its Human Resources Planning and Development ("Flextime" 1981).

HOW TO IMPLEMENT FLEXTIME

Merck points out five basic steps involved in implementing flextime:

- selection of a divisional (or location) flextime coordinator
- management (departmental) analysis to determine feasibility of implementing flextime
- information provided to managers on the concept, procedures, scheduling approaches, and other guidelines for successful flextime implementation
- supervisory meetings with employees to review flextime guidelines and procedures
- employee selection of schedules, management review, and approval of schedule selection

Now we can look at these guidelines in some detail.

SELECTING A COORDINATOR

Merck's management believes that while a flextime coordinator's job is not particularly demanding, it is essential. The coordinator's responsibilities include arranging briefings with local managers so they understand how to implement flextime. He or she also provides these local managers with guidelines for conducting information sessions with their employees. The coordinator also continues to act as the contact person and source of information on any problems that occur when implementing flextime. This individual also is the contact person with whom corporate human resources or others can discuss issues that might occur.

Merck notes that the coordinator is primarily needed in the initial month of flextime implementation ("Flextime" 1981). In its experience, the flextime coordinator's role is minimal after the initial implementation phase. There will probably always be a need for some central coordination. Deciding when and where, as well as where not, to implement flextime is the subject of the rest of the chapter. We will also look specifically at how to set up a flextime program.

DETERMINING FEASIBILITY

Before implementing flextime, you should carefully analyze the pros and cons of using it. This thorough analysis of flextime potential in your work area is essential before trying to implement the plan in your location.

The responsibility for assessing this feasibility usually rests with the departmental managers, since they are the ones who are directly affected. While each manager must make the decision whether to use or not to use it, Merck points out that it has found very few departments where flextime is inappropriate or difficult to implement but reminds us that implementing flextime can present some problems and challenges.

One of these challenges to implementing flextime is its effect on departmental operations. In fact, the company notes that flextime can be difficult to implement if your department is very small. Smaller departments are much more interdependent and require closer coordination. Second, flextime can be more difficult to implement, although obviously not impossible, if a department requires a full staff of employees during the normal eight-hour day to service its clients adequately. Departments that require high coordination or interaction throughout the day can also cause some problems. Likewise, departments that have a continuous operation with shift work can pose problems.

All of this discussion is not to imply that flextime cannot be implemented if these conditions exist, only that they create some administrative problems that must be dealt with. A department that has all four of these characteristics provides the greatest challenge. On the other hand, Merck emphasizes that departments without any of these four characteristics should have few problems. For any department, flextime offers some major benefits.

In assessing whether flextime is appropriate or not, consider a couple of issues. The first of these is the effect of absenteeism on your department. In other words, is the absence of some employees during early or late hours of the day going to cause serious problems? If there are some problems, how will you provide full service to your customers? This issue must be answered before flextime can be set up.

Second, ask yourself if there are any benefits to your department from using flextime. These might include longer utilization of equipment or early preparation of work on which your internal or external customers depend. Situations like these make flextime a natural. You also want to make sure your department is large enough to assure you have your work activities covered during all phases of the normal workday.

Merck adds that when you do this feasibility study, two guidelines should underlie your use of flextime. One of these is that the use of flextime and selection of production schedules should always be based on the production needs of your department. Management's primary responsibility is to make sure production needs are met and flextime must always take a backseat to those needs.

The second guideline is for the department manager to keep veto power over employee selection of work schedules. The reason is that it is sometimes necessary for a particular employee or employees to be at work at specific times of the workday. For most organizations, full customer service, along with productivity, is a top priority. As such, it prevents all employees from fully participating in flextime.

Basic information on how to implement flextime should be reviewed with everyone who will be affected before it is implemented. It is usually the responsibility of the flextime coordinator to provide information on the disadvantages and advantages of flextime. The coordinator should also review schedules, record keeping procedures, and approaches one could use. There should be discussions of any problems or other special concerns or questions department managers may have.

DISADVANTAGES

There are drawbacks to flextime, some of which are obvious. For instance, there may be some decrease in availability of some employees. Whenever there is a flextime system, naturally employees will be coming in at different times. You will need to know their schedule rather than assuming they will always be there.

It is also possible (especially without good planning) that flextime could adversely affect the availability of your support services, if they are also using flextime. Depending on your department, this support structure could be anything from medical services to typing and other office services. The effect of flextime on such support is a key to being able to use flextime.

Naturally, there may also be some decreased scheduling flexibility since some people may not be at the workplace at certain times. It will be important to make sure, from an operational point of view, that there is not substantially reduced employee coverage of critical work. Administratively, more effort will be needed to keep track of the employee work time. It can be noted, though, that many companies using flextime depend on peer pressure to take care of cheaters.

Another disadvantage might be that those who cannot participate in flextime can become dissatisfied. Although this disadvantage cannot always be eliminated, it can be reduced by good planning on the part of management and good preparation of the work force. Obviously, there are advantages to flextime that can more than offset the disadvantages.

ADVANTAGES

Merck says there can be advantages for both employees and managers. From the employees' viewpoint, it allows them the opportunity to adjust their work schedule to suit them better. After all, not all people work best on a traditional 8 to 5 schedule. We have all heard of people who describe themselves as "morning" people or "night" people. Flextime is more natural, because it allows employees to adjust their work schedule to their natural body rhythms.

Flextime makes it easier for employees to attend to personal matters since many services are open primarily during the normal workday. Having some flexibility when one comes to work not only diminishes personal scheduling problems but also diminishes other problems like traffic congestion. Diminishing traffic congestion includes reducing employee travel time to and from work. For many, this produces a better work environment because it reduces stress normally associated with having to drive to work during peak commuting hours. If it is possible to eliminate some of the tension and anxiety that employees feel before and after they leave work, then chances are you will help increase their job satisfaction. Time not spent traveling can be spent at work or play. Part of flextime's power is its ability to give employees a greater sense of personal responsibility, freedom, and opportunity for participation in decision making. Deciding when to come and leave work is part of that decision making.

So far all the discussion has centered on employees, but they are not the only ones to reap the advantages of flextime. Managers also have some strong reasons to consider using flextime. Foremost among these advantages is improved employee morale. If your employees are happier with their work arrangement, then your job as a manager is easier.

Happiness does not necessarily mean increased productivity. What is flextime's effect on productivity? Merck believes that flextime has improved its employees' work performance ("Flextime" 1981). It also reports decreased single-day absenteeism, as well as elimination of employee tardiness and decreased requests for personal time off. Merck also reports that employees are more task-oriented rather than time-oriented.

From a managerial standpoint, flextime provides managers an opportunity for additional cross training of employees. Since employees come and go at different times within the workday, it is sometimes necessary for employees to be able to do several things so they can cover for those who are not there. Cross training itself, as we shall see, brings enormous advantages to a company, not the least of which are increased speed and flexibility.

Perhaps surprisingly, flextime can also result in a decrease in overtime. The reason is that the organization is more flexible, because people work different lengths of time. Since employees work different schedules, it is quite likely that somebody will be available when extra work is needed, making it unnecessary to work overtime.

Finally, one additional advantage of flextime involves employees' maturity and control, including their improved management of their time. Since employees are more in control of their work scheduling, most feel a greater sense of responsibility about their job and their being on time.

MERCK'S FLEXTIME

In the next few pages, we shall review Merck's particular approach to flextime. Obviously, each industry and each company should adjust these guidelines to suit their own particular needs. Merck's system has three definitions worth noting. Core time is a designated time during which all employees must be on the job. FST stands for flexible start time and is the range of times in which employees are able to begin work. FQT stands for flexible quit time and refers to discretionary time in which employees are able to end the workday ("Flextime" 1981).

Employees are expected to work their normal eight-hour workday during each five-day week. The core time for all employees is between 9:30 A.M. and 3:30 P.M. FSTs range from 7:00 A.M. to 9:30 A.M., and FQTs range from 3:30 P.M. to 6:00 P.M. Merck notes that discretionary time does not mean that such time is unplanned. Employees must schedule their starting and quitting times, and their work times must meet the needs of the department.

Employees must also secure the approval of their managers to help ensure their jobs are adequately covered. To help ensure stability, employees maintain their work schedule for at least one week. To improve coordination, Merck posts work schedules of employees in the work area, so all are aware of the availability of specific people.

Flexibility does not mean there is no control. Even with flextime, lateness is not acceptable, and anyone who is late should have a good reason. Any lateness should be made up. Normal overtime rules should be in effect. For these reasons you need to keep good records.

RECORD KEEPING

The first rule about flextime record keeping is to keep it simple. Use a simple approach both to record and to display schedules of all employees. As noted earlier, simple schedules should be developed on a weekly basis. A sample schedule is seen in Figure 8.1. Such schedules should be displayed in areas accessible to everyone who can be affected by them. Management should keep records of these schedules for one year. Merck says this retention helps managers review employee behavior under flextime and decide on any changes that may be needed.

No other additional flextime reports are needed, but it will be necessary to keep your normal records on employee absences and tardiness.

Figure 8.1
Flextime Work Schedule

DEPARTMENT _____   WEEK OF _____

EMPLOYEE NAME	STARTING TIME	QUITTING TIME
1.		
2.		
3.		
4.		
5.		
6.		
7.		
8.		
9.		
10.		
11.		
12.		
13.		
14.		
15.		
16.		
17.		

Source: Courtesy of Merck & Company

If you do not normally keep such records, it is a good idea to do so under flextime. During the first six months keep track of any problems that occur in implementing flextime.

SUPERVISORY MEETINGS

After departmental managers have made an analysis of the feasibility of flextime, they will decide whether or not to use it. If the decision has been made to use it, they will then need to meet with departmental employees. At these meetings, departmental managers announce that flextime, where feasible, will be held. During these meetings, these managers review the advantages and drawbacks of flextime that were already mentioned in this chapter. At this time, it is also good to review the basic guidelines and procedures for posting work schedules. Naturally, these meetings should include an open discussion with employees about flextime.

During these supervisory meetings several points should be made. It should be made clear to employees that any work schedules always must fit within the production needs of the department. The point should be made that some people may not be able to participate fully because certain work must occur during the normal work hours. Adequate coverage is essential; the use of flextime is secondary.

Everyone in these meetings should understand that it must ultimately be the responsibility of departmental managers to decide when and to what degree flextime can be used in their departments. Furthermore, make sure they understand that this is an experiment and that after a period of time, if it appears it is inappropriate, it may be necessary to return to "normal" work hours.

CONCLUDING THOUGHTS

The decision that you and your company make to implement flextime should be based on whether it allows you a chance to adopt to changing life-styles and employee needs. It probably will be welcomed by those employees who have two-income families and others who need the additional flexibility of flextime. Some say the only reason it is suspect is that men do not use it. For example, only 2 percent of eligible men have used unpaid parental leaves, but, increasingly, even they are starting to change (Deutschman 1991). Flextime has often produced improved productivity and employee morale, but only if it is properly managed. It is important for a manager who wishes to use some form of flextime to negotiate a clearly defined set of responsibilities rather than simply fix the days or hours when employees will work. Otherwise, star performers can easily get stuck with a 100 percent load in a 60 percent time slot (Deutschman 1991). Merck's managers believe it benefits both them and their employees but must realistically decide if it is appropriate for them.

Your ability to implement flextime is, in large part, dependent on your employees' ability to be self-managed, as well as on your preparation and training. Flextime shifts the responsibility more toward employees and, obviously, depends on each employee's dependability. Before you implement flextime, each employee must be prepared for the flexibility as well as the accountability being established. Next, we will look at ways of increasing employee preparation and value to the company. Such preparation not only helps implement flextime but also greatly increases one's ability to retain and enhance employee relations.

REFERENCES

Baumann, M. "Cart Titled Family Business." *News-Leader*, November 26, 1990, D1.

Deutschman, Alan. "Pioneers of the New Balance." *Fortune*, May 20, 1991, 60–68.

Flextime Implementation Guidelines. Merck's Human Resources Planning and Development, February 1981.

Hewlett, William R. "The Human Side of Management." *Eugene B. Clark Executive Lecture*, University of Notre Dame, March 25, 1982, 9.

9

Building A Culture

While just about every company is interested in recruiting, retaining, and improving employee relations, some manage these activities more easily than others do. Their success in this area is no accident. They have a corporate culture that generates its own human resource success. American Express provides us with an excellent example of a positive culture creating a positive human resource.

Every culture has to have a central theme, something that makes the company distinctive. The center of the culture at American Express is a focus on the customer. The customer as the centerpiece of the company is a philosophy that is understood by all managers and employees. Anything, any process or technique, that contributes to better customer relations is of interest. Unlike most companies, American Express's concern for the customer is more than talk. As we shall see, it set up a system to make sure everyone buys its cultural focus.

At American Express this cultural concern for the customer's viewpoint is the key to its motivational efforts. MaryAnne Rasmussen, the then vice president of Worldwide Quality Assurance for American Express's Travel Related Service (their credit card business), says, *'Employees can only be motivated when they clearly understand the impact of what they do, and when they value their part in the service or product they deliver''* (Rasmussen 1988, 12).

Putting the customer at the center of one's culture is not the only way to enhance employee performance and relations, but it helps. Some companies use the budget, some use a participatory goal-setting process, and some even use the inherent value of the service provided as their focal point. Regardless of the focus, it is essential for management first to identify what is important before trying to improve relations with, and performance of, employees.

American Express's managers chose the customer and, more specifically, quality service to their customers as their central theme, which has worked very well for them. Rasmussen believes one of the reasons it has worked so well is that employees can easily put themselves in the customer's shoes and, in the process, take pride in doing a job well done. She says that pride in one's own performance gives everyone a sense of purpose (Rasmussen 1988) and that the company's culture motivates its employees. In turn, motivated employees are able to deliver the quality the company needs to remain competitive.

INFRASTRUCTURE

Since the culture of American Express and the corresponding ability to create pride and motivation are interrelated, it is important to look at several elements that make up its process for creating both of these. The first of these elements for creating a motivating culture is its Quality Assurance Organization, which provides the necessary infrastructure to support motivational efforts.

The centerpiece of this infrastructure is Quality Assurance Centers located in every one of its worldwide operations centers. American Express's operations centers are its central administrative areas, and each of these Quality Assurance Departments reports directly to the CEO of these centers. Access to, and support of, the CEO are essential, support from the CEO provides legitimacy and shows everyone the corporation's priorities. Few within American Express do not know what is near and dear to the CEO's heart. All employees understand the focus of their jobs and that of the corporation. In American Express's case, this focus is quality assurance. Everyone knows because of its structure and quality activities that quality assurance is as important as sales or marketing. That importance is something most services do not recognize. Support of the CEO, a system that ties quality assurance directly to the CEO, and activities that emphasize corporate objectives of quality assurance are all part of the operational infrastructure.

How does quality assurance affect employee motivation and employee relations? Part of the infrastructure is its training programs. It is not enough to know something is important, to the CEO and corporation is general. It is not enough to have a desire to participate; one must also know how to contribute and be trained how to do it.

TRAINING

American Express gives employees the means as well as motivation to contribute through its training efforts. The important point, though, is not that it provides training but rather that this training gives employees a means of learning about their business. This is a point worth emphasizing.

It is not necessarily critical that every organization emphasize quality to have a competitive culture and a motivated work force. The important point is that every organization needs some vehicle for employees to learn about their corporation and the importance of their own jobs to the health of that business. Later, we will look at one company that uses open disclosure of financial numbers and then makes everyone from vice presidents to janitors accountable for those numbers. There are other equally effective operational systems that can be used to teach employees about their own contribution and the importance of their jobs.

While there are other operational systems besides quality assurance that can be used, American Express does an excellent job of using it to enhance its employee relations and motivation. Rasmussen makes the same point when she notes that through its coordinated quality assurance efforts employees are able to *see first-hand how one aspect of the business or process affects another* (Rasmussen 1988, 15). The company shows them the relevance of their jobs. By showing its line people how to improve their services, thereby increasing revenue and reducing expenses. This broader perspective is essential to good employee relations and motivation.

In their training sessions American Express managers also try to knock down walls. In line with this holistic view, they make sure trainees do not just look at what sales or data processing or accounting or even customer service does. Rather, they try to have everyone look at the total business operation. In this process, people learn about the business and its needs and the interdependence of each other.

This holism is a critical ingredient. If we, as a nation, are going to be able to retain employees and improve relations with them, it is essential for managers to find ways of creating this integrated understanding of their business. American Express is able to do this through the work of its Quality Assurance Centers.

Rasmussen says centers provide training programs so everyone understands the overall business. She also notes that such training prepares participants for advancement. Those people who work with the quality assurance (Q.A.) staff learn the effect their performance has, not just on their customers but, most importantly, on their colleagues.

Developing a greater understanding and appreciation of one's impact on others is another key to employee motivation and enhancement of relations within the entire organization. Think about it. It is often surprising how few of us really do know whom we serve and who serves us. Few of us know what others want, and fewer still know what others truly need from us. Far too many people see themselves as a piece in a never-ending puzzle, a cog in the machinery. What is worse is that they cannot even understand the machinery and why certain things are done. Our job as managers is continuously to show others where they relate and the relevance of their work.

TRACKING

Clearly, American Express has a system (by emphasizing quality service) that provides employees with an understanding of how a business works and their corresponding effect upon others. Impressive as this system is, it is not enough simply to create an understanding and appreciation within the work force. One also needs to find a way of evaluating employees' efforts so corrections can be made.

American Express further focuses its employees' interest and efforts through the second element of its Q.A., namely, tracking. In any good motivational system, it is essential to have some way to track employee performance. American Express's tracking system is legendary. It literally uses hundreds of quality standards to track the performance of its personnel. The system measures and monitors the quality of the service it delivers and so ensures the critical linkage between effort and results.

American Express refers to the tracking system as Service Tracking Reports. It is in place worldwide and measures those things that relate to its goal of customer service. These tracking systems include measuring the time it takes to process new applications, to bill card members, and to respond to card members' inquiries. This and similar types of measurements of performance on a monthly basis are evaluated, analyzed, and reviewed by management.

A critical aspect of the tracking system is that management review comes from the very top. Jim Robinson, American Express's CEO, and other top managers regularly review their key performance standards. Thus, operational details are not delegated to strictly lower levels. Of equal importance to this top management commitment is the fact that the results of these reviews are shared with all employees. Making this link between performance and results helps employees see how they and their team perform (Rasmussen 1988).

American Express notes that when its measurement system in in place, dramatic improvements are achieved. Employees begin offering new ideas and approaches, thus creating a momentum of its own.

LINKAGES

The third way American Express creates the motivation necessary to ensure a viable culture is through the linkages it establishes. Specifically, it tries to link an individual's efforts and those results that affect the bottom line. For instance, American Express pioneered the use of the transaction-based survey. As the name implies, surveys are used to evaluate individual transactions between specific service providers and their individual customers. Unlike typical market research that collects demographics, they actually try to measure the results of individual transactions between specific employees and customers.

The survey of individual transactions asks customers if they felt the service representative was courteous, competent, and knowledgeable and if they were satisfied with the results of their transaction.

American Express believes these individual transaction-based surveys are great employee motivational tools because they link employee efforts and their affect upon the customer a one-on-one proposition. Employees can read questionnaire responses directly from specific customers whom they served. Such direct feedback makes the job they do even more real because employees are able to see their individual contribution.

Making this link between individual effort and individual customers is another one of the keys to good motivation and enhanced relations with employees. This linkage, in American Express's case, involves linking individual effort and individual customers. It is a good link, but not necessarily the only way to link performance and results. Other companies tie corporate profitability, quality, or productivity to individual efforts. Regardless of the content of the linkage, it is necessary to establish these linkages if performance and employee relations are to be improved. Most managers are never truly able to establish these linkages for their employees. If employees do not know the specific relevance of the specific jobs they do, how can we expect them to be productive? The great companies and the great managers can specifically point out exactly what the costs are and the reasons we must do our job to the best of our ability.

REVIEWS AND FEEDBACK

The fourth way American Express has been able to build a competitive culture is through extensive formal and informal on-site performance review. The heart of this review process is a method that Hewlett-Packard made famous, namely, Management-by-Wandering-Around (MBWA). American Express strongly recommends that all of their managers spend time with their employees. American Express managers spend time asking their employees what customers are saying to them and, just as importantly, what they think should be done to improve their operation.

Rasmussen believes MBWA gives employees a great sense of fulfillment to have their boss sincerely ask their opinion about how to improve work or relations with the customer. American Express combines these informal MBWA interviews with on-site management reviews where teams of corporate staff visit employees at their various operations centers.

The goal of these teams is to raise employee awareness of their corporate goals and techniques. They do this in part by reviewing customer service inquiries. The objective of the discussion is to find out what is needed by their employees to enable them to perform their job better. American Express hopes the message its employees get from MBWA and on-site interviews is that employee ideas are critical to the company's success.

ATTITUDINAL TRAINING

Another reason American Express is able to motivate its people and improve its quality is its employee educational process. Management spends a great deal of money and time on training and development. As already noted, training includes helping employees better understand the company perspective as well as the traditional training of showing them how to do their job better. This training includes concentrating on their individual and problem-solving skills.

Rasmussen emphasizes that the most challenging part of the company's training efforts involved trying to build a "network of employees who have the same attitudes and philosophy about their corporate objectives" (Rasmussen 1988). To this end, management constantly tries to have employees not only buy into the process (in this case, the process of quality improvement) but also "embrace it, improve it, and turn it into a way of life of their own" (Rasmussen 1988, 14).

Such attitudinal training is far from pie-in-the-sky thinking. American Express believes it is critical to its ability to remain productive. For this reason it has spent a lot of effort developing local, regional, and companywide programs for that purpose.

There are many such programs, one of which is called "Putting People First." It is a two-day seminar designed to improve everyone's sensitivity to his or her respective customers. Typically, in each session these meetings include about 100 people from entry-level employees to vice presidents.

The emphasis is on feeling better about yourself, knowing how you want to be treated, and then treating your internal and external customers the same way. These attitude adjustment sessions attempt to improve not only attitudes of individuals but also their teams' attitudes. What attitudes are they talking about, and what themes do they use?

Rasmussen says that American Express feels that Robert Darwin, the CEO of Scandinavian Design Inc., said it best: "There is only one thing that counts in a business—building the self-esteem of your employees. Nothing else matters because what they feel about themselves is what they give your customers" (Rasmussen 1988). The point is that if employees come to work not liking it and not feeling good about themselves, then your customers will probably go away not feeling good about your company.

EI

Part of American Express's ability to create a vital culture comes through its employee involvement (EI) activities. There is nothing particularly magical here. The company uses traditional techniques; the difference is that it uses them more extensively than most. For instance, it recognizes outstanding employee performance throughout the company. It has developed over 100 different reward, recognition, suggestion, and communication programs. Some are tailored to specific countries; other are companywide.

One example of a very successful EI program is its "Great Performer's Award," which honors individual employees around the world who have performed feats that go above and beyond the call of duty. American Express's management sees the awards as a kind of Academy Award for service. Winners are flown to New York, wined, dined, and given cash awards at a banquet attended by top executives. The company publicizes all this celebration in corporate literature worldwide.

Rasmussen gives an example of one such "great performer," an employee in Salt Lake City who spoke German to a distraught, non-English-speaking Dutch tourist in the United States. She had been robbed of her traveler's checks, receipts, passport, plane tickets, driver's license, and car rental contract. The employee immediately arranged for a refund for the traveler's checks, got her a new rental contract, had new travel papers and passport issued, arranged for new airline tickets, and got the tourist home. Now, that's service!

While the company makes use of corporatewide programs like its Great Performer's Award, it also recognizes that local areas should develop their own rewards that suit local needs, so local managers have their own recognition activities for their employees; sometimes they are quite extensive.

One such case involves an operations center in Florida. At this center, managers hold regular weekly meetings where the local senior vice president recognizes employees in front of their colleagues. At the same location, they have a "Quality Awareness" month. During this month, executives take outstanding work units to dinner at first-class restaurants. Raffle tickets are sold, and parties are given each week with prizes awarded to top performers. These prizes are not necessarily insignificant or just tokens; some have included trips for two to California and the Bahamas.

This same center also has a Quality Club with lunches, pins, and certificates for exceptionally high performance and employees-of-the-month commendations. Again, the EI rewards are not necessarily that unusual—just extensive!

COMMUNICATION

Communication, like rewards, does not have to be different to be effective. It is how you make use of the tool that counts, not how novel it is. Much of American Express's ability to motivate and maintain good employee relations rests on its ability to communicate. This includes keeping employees updated on new activities, products, initiatives, advertising, and strategies it is planning to use. Its annual report also informs employees about accomplishments of the previous year and its upcoming goals and plans.

Management makes extensive use of videotapes and, whenever possible, teleconferences. It uses these tools to keep employees informed about any significant aspects, influencing new products it might be planning to use. It also uses traditional newsletters to keep its people informed about what is going on.

The goal of all of these tools is to keep employees enthusiastic and involved. Management sees one of its primary roles as recognizing outstanding employees. It hopes to develop pride not only in employees but in their teammates as well. In other words, it does not simply manage, but rather leads.

LEADERSHIP

No discussion of motivation would be complete without a discussion of leadership, which determines how to motivate others and how to build team pride. Rasmussen says great leaders believe what they say and say exactly what is on their minds. She emphasizes that they inspire loyalty and trust, because they deliver what they promise (Rasmussen 1988).

Such leadership takes a commitment to excellence, and it appears that American Express's CEO, Jim Robinson, has that commitment. He has a commitment and emphasis on quality. When *Forbes*, in its annual survey of the most promising people in corporate America, asked Robinson what he believed his greatest career achievement was, he said it was an emphasis on quality: "I want quality written on my tombstone" (Rasmussen 1988). Now, that's commitment. Of course, commitment alone is not enough. Many believe it is Robinson's ability to select and support other senior managers who are equally committed to quality that has been a large part of American Express's success (Rasmussen 1988).

CONCLUDING THOUGHTS

One final point needs to be made about American Express's culture and its approach to employee motivation. Rasmussen says she read a letter from an employee that told her a lot. In this letter, the employee said, "It is great working for a company that cares about its people"; this employee felt happy and proud to be working for a company that is respected for the quality of its products and services (Rasmussen 1988).

When you have the majority of your people feeling this way, you will not have trouble creating good employee relations and a viable and dynamic culture. Rasmussen points out that people want to give their best and that management's job is to encourage employees and then empower them so they can give their best. In succeeding chapters, we will look at ways we can help people give their best.

REFERENCE

Rasmussen, MaryAnne E. "American Express: Quality Culture Our Key to Motivating Employees." *American Productivity and Quality Center Executive Center*, August 4, 1988.

10

Competitive Culture: The Story of Fujitsu

The word *world-class* has been overused. Some people use it the way those in Hollywood use the term *star*; even those with minor credits and accomplishments can call themselves stars. The same is true of those who use the term *world-class competitor*. Many minor league companies mistakenly claim they are world-class simply because they export; this status, however, requires a track record of successful global competition, excelling, and market share power. Motorola is a world-class competitor, along with General Electric and American Express. They are all well known in the United States and worldwide. America, though, is not the only country with world-class, superstar companies.

Fujitsu Limited, a Japanese-owned company, also seems to fit the bill as a world-class company. Despite the lack of exposure in the United States, Fujitsu has been around for some time. It was established in 1935 and today is Japan's number one computer company. It is a world leader in the manufacture of computer-related technology, like data processing, communication systems, semiconductors, and other electrical components. The company employs over 145,872 people worldwide and has annual sales of over $21 billion.

In the 1950s, the company began research into the field of semiconductors. In 1956, it was the first in Japan to apply computer technology to numerically controlled machines. More recently, it has developed a variety of office automation equipment, including word processors, personal computers, workstations, and facsimile equipment.

Fujitsu's overseas market has expanded to include subsidiaries and manufacturing facilities around the globe. The stereotype of efficient Japanese who lack inventiveness and originality does not apply to Fujitsu. By any standards, much of its technology is leading edge. For instance, it is currently developing a visual movement controller that makes use of artificial intelligence (AI) by using "ultrafast moving processing and fuzzy inference." Translation: it is developing a visual system that will be the eyes of intelligent robots that recognize shapes and colors of objects and then can make decisions about specific conditions. Its system already has been successfully tested in driverless automobiles that can negotiate turns and avoid obstacles in their path!

Being a so-called high-tech star does not mean it has forgotten what led to its success. While much of what it sells is hardware, it still places its managerial emphasis on people. Despite the glamour of high tech, it keeps two goals in mind that it believes keep it a world-class competitor.

A fundamental principle of its success is management's desire to keep the company highly streamlined. Its objective is to control the corporate bureaucracy so it does not interfere with its people. In a moment, we will look at how it does this. Second, like many American companies, it is continuously trying to keep its people empowered—but with a decidedly Japanese flavor.

While many teams want to win and many companies want to be more competitive, few actually are world-class. Fujitsu's goals are not that foreign to American thinking. They could be the goals of any aspiring, upstart company. It is not so much Fujitsu's goals as it is its ability to execute those plans that has led to its success. It is in an almost continuous state of organizational fine-tuning (sometimes a major overhaul is needed) of its performance. It wants to maintain an entrepreneurial drive and spirit of start-up companies. Interjecting this entrepreneurial spirit within this mammoth organization is the real secret of its success and of its competitive culture.

RINGI SYSTEM

For a mature organization like Fujitsu to remain competitive year after year, it feels that it is essential to overcome those problems often associated with big companies. It feels innovation and an aggressive, competitive attitude helped make it successful. Bureaucracy and bigness can soon snuff out such competitive fires and lead to a lack of initiative. To stay fresh and avoid doing things in entrenched ways, it tries to avoid doing something just because "that's the way it's always been done."

Most companies in Japan use something called the "Ringi System" which means "request for authority." Fujitsu streamlined it and eliminated some red tape and paperwork normally associated with management by consensus. Fujitsu has streamlined and simplified its ringi system, including reducing the number of approvals necessary to take action. As part of this process, it has also eliminated all ongoing expenditures from its system and significantly raised the minimum expenditure level needed for special requests. Red tape and bureaucracy are discouraged. One way it does this is for requests to be limited to one page. These requests must also be clearly written and easily understandable. Excessive use of appendixes and attachments is strongly discouraged.

SUBSIDIARY EXISTENCE

A majority of Fujitsu employees work in the industrial sector. Because of its greater size, there is an especially high risk of excessive organizational complexity and bureaucracy. The company diminishes the effect of size and its accompanying bureaucracy, which stifles the entrepreneurial spirit, by setting up profit centers for all of its product divisions and subsidiaries. In a departure from traditional American thinking, these profit centers also include R&D subsidiaries. Fujitsu subsidiaries are the primary form of organization, and there are more employees in them than in the actual parent company. The parent company has only about 50,768 of its total of 145,872 employees; the rest are employed in subsidiaries.

A "focused factory" mentality is also the reason the company keeps those operations, which are out of Fujitsu's mainstream, as separate subsidiaries. Top-level management is convinced that each entity should have its own culture.

Fujitsu Limited believes that encouraging an entrepreneurial spirit means that each of its 150 subsidiaries and affiliated companies should have its own personality. To achieve this, Fujitsu Limited gives its affiliated companies a wide latitude in operational freedom and autonomy. It feels such an approach encourages an entrepreneurial spirit and helps the subsidiaries fine-tune appropriate market approaches for each subsidiary's specific business. It refers to this concept as "Think global, act local."

THINK GLOBAL, ACT LOCAL

There are many definitions of this phrase, but at Fujitsu it refers to its arm's-length policy toward its worldwide subsidiary operations, including Fujitsu America, Australia, and Europe. Each of these subsidiaries is run as a local company. The Japanese parent company does allocate resources and engages in joint operations and technology exchange, but the independence of the company is highly prized.

An example of this philosophy was seen when Fujitsu made an 80 percent capital investment in ICL of Great Britain and Fujitsu's chairman,

Yamomoto, publicly promised to maintain this arm's-length management policy. The goal of such an approach is to have subsidiaries benefit from their association with the parent organization without having to look to headquarters for authority to do something. The attitude seems to be that as long as managers are successful, there is no reason to interfere. Fujitsu reasons that local management is in the best position to judge local markets and local conditions. It carries this philosophy one step further by also including its R&D efforts in this decentralized approach. It feels it is impossible for a designer in Tokyo to know what is best for European or American markets.

Fujitsu's far-flung R&D centers from Richardson, Texas, to Middlesex, England, epitomize the phrase "Think global, act local." Diversified R&D facilities give the strategic advantage of a cross-cultural exchange among researchers of different nationalities. Technical synergy comes from facilities like its all-American memory storage subsidiary, called Intellistar, working with its Japanese counterparts.

This cross-cultural exchange not only increases synergy but can also reap other advantages. There are advantages for customers since they have locally designed and engineered products. In turn, greater customer appeal helps Fujitsu remain more competitive.

TOTAL PROJECT INVOLVEMENT

Cross-cultural exchanges and extensive use of subsidiaries are not the only ways Fujitsu tries to instill an entrepreneurial spirit within the company. Its approach toward projects also gives it a competitive advantage. Special projects at Fujitsu are a big deal. The company encourages all sections and divisions, including those within its headquarters, and its subsidiaries to choose independently an "exciting project or service" on which to concentrate.

What is unique about this approach is not the suggestion about choosing a special project to champion, but rather the control and authority these project managers exercise over their projects. The hope is that every manager, particularly so-called XXX project managers (their equivalent of our Project Champions), who are not tied to a specific division, can exercise personal control over both project development and production.

An illustration of this tactic can be seen with a project involving a new type of semiconductor device called the Josephson Junction. The company believes the device will operate 100 times faster than conventional computers. As one might expect, the project manager's personal involvement in the Josephson Junction project is extensive. However, what might not be expected is his involvement with all aspects of the project. He not only does the traditional R&D work but also will follow the project from the R&D subsidiary through the semiconductor division and even see his technology introduced to market.

This total involvement in all phases of the project is not an isolated incident for Fujitsu. Each year it has about 50 researchers carrying their R&D projects through to their respective product divisions. Thus, researchers see their technology come to commercial fruition. Researchers are even encouraged to see their projects to the marketplace and are given the necessary control, money, and other incentives to see it happen. In fact, Fujitsu notes that many of its researchers do not return to the lab for some time—if at all! It emphasizes that in Japan, unlike in America, production is more highly regarded than pure research. Many of the Japanese researchers consider being involved in these production aspects as a reward rather than something to be avoided. There is a strategic advantage when researchers do not mind "getting their hands dirty" with the day-to-day production aspects of their project and do not think of themselves as superior to production.

EMPOWERMENT—FUJITSU STYLE

Japanese companies are best known for their incremental improvements rather than revolutionary advances. Today, many Japanese companies believe they must find ways of encouraging innovation or else always play the role of catching up. A lack of innovation, however, is not a characteristic of Fujitsu. Among other accomplishments, it has credit for many advances, including the world's fastest main frames and the smallest cellular phone. It is also the inventor of the High Electron Mobility Transistor (HEMT) and a 70 percent market share of the superfast communications receiver market. It believes one day soon HEMT will mean it will be able to bring supercomputer speed down to lap size.

Managers at Fujitsu believe they are able to innovate in large part because of their philosophy of "One man can make great things happen." The company believes that the talents of a single person, if cultivated and allowed to blossom, could yield far more results than teams of researchers working on projects. Perhaps this attitude is due to its experience with former Fujitsu's president, Kanjiro Okado, who is credited for almost single-handedly applying the company's communication technology to the field of computers. Because of Mr. Okada's determination, the company was responsible for building Japan's first commercial computers. He also helped focus the company on the information-processing area, which today accounts for 70 percent of its business.

Perhaps this example shows why the company believes that the talents of one man can create great things. Its experience with Okado is probably one of the reasons it believes in R&D subsidiary research rather than a more centralized approach. The rationale is that subsidiary R&D create more opportunities for the talents of the individual to be recognized.

So much for the myth that Japan is a homogeneous culture where the individual is subverted for the good of the team. It is true it has team players, but it appears, at least in Fujitsu's case, that the power of the individual is highly prized.

ONE-THIRD RULE

Each subsidiary of the company is expected to apply Fujitsu's philosophy of cross-application of technology. The aim is to allow researchers to work in areas not directly related to their immediate product development. The company believes such an approach enhances the chances of innovation and diminishes the interdivisional rivalry that can delay projects. This cross-application philosophy can also be traced to Okada's personal work practice of not only handling his "assigned" projects but also assisting other work groups with their work-in-process.

An example of this cross-application approach involves Fujitsu Laboratories, which is a wholly owned subsidiary of the parent company. The lab's current president, Masaki Ogi, follows this approach, which he calls the "One-Third Rule." This one-third rule means that of the total work performed at the lab, in terms of budget allocation, one-third is based directly on contracts from headquarters, one-third is related to particular products, and one-third is reserved for pure or "basic" research. This policy is impressive, considering the lab is a profit center. The purpose of the one-third percentages is for the lab to keep attracting contract business (since it is a profit center), as well as work on breakthrough technologies.

One of the company's most famous breakthroughs for this one-third rule was its development of the HEMT device, a new type of semiconductor that is used in microwave transmission and as a receiver for direct satellite broadcast systems in Japan. HEMT has exceptional "sensitivity" and enables the company to shrink fully functioning satellite dishes to 35 centimeters, small enough for you to set on the television itself or mount on the veranda. The company also believes this exciting technology will play an important role in future generations of computers.

The interesting aspect of HEMT is that it was not even a project that the company had assigned to anyone. It was not even a project at all. Rather, it was primarily the idea of one man, Dr. Mimura, who at the time was working on another assignment. It was pure research; there was no evidence that his idea would bear fruit, but he was given the freedom to explore the idea. A small team of three to five engineers was made available to assist on the project, but it was mostly Dr. Mimura's project. The one-third rule evolved from experience with the HEMT project.

Mimura's project also shows the power that project managers exercise within Fujitsu. Mimura told his section leader what was needed. He then helped develop plans and schedules to be followed by his section leader. Contrary to traditional American approaches, Mimura's plans were to be followed by management and not simply submitted to it. The rationale was that the researcher, not general management, was in the best position to judge how fast or slow the project would proceed through the phases of design, development, and eventual fabrication and testing.

Today, the lab continues to try to cultivate the same type of freedom and project authority that led to Mimura's success. To this end, all researchers are encouraged to have pet projects to work on in their spare time. Once researchers believe they have done the necessary basic research on their private project, they present it to the company and ask to work on it full-time. Most of these requests are granted because the company believes breakthroughs come when people are personally interested in something rather than simply assigned to a project.

UNIQUE TEAMS

Fujitsu's worldwide and decentralized approach has given it a unique perspective. One of the key insights it has developed is that creativity and synergy are enhanced by forming groups of unique composition. For instance, it has had great success, both in Japan and in its overseas operations, at using intercultural teams.

Fujitsu is convinced that Japanese and non-Japanese researches, working together, are able to benefit from each other's unique ways of thinking about particular subjects. In its Japanese laboratories, there are full-time employees working alongside employees from nearly a hundred countries. This intercultural teamwork is in addition to the temporary researchers it uses from its overseas subsidiaries, affiliates, and even personnel from its customers' companies (e.g., MCI, U.S. West, Siemens AG, etc.), as well as personnel from Manchester, Australian National University, Harvard, MIT, and Queens University in Belfast. Fujitsu does admit that communication and differences in culture can sometimes be difficult. While this may be the case, its work teams have universally reported that they benefited from the interaction of these cross-cultural groups.

Intercultural teams are a big part of Fujitsu's success in the world marketplace. It has also found that setting up other unique groups can be highly successful. The personal characteristics of different groups can be used to their advantage. Fujitsu has been successful at forming research groups by age, sex, and field of study. It has also discovered that existing research groups can benefit from those graduates who are fresh out of school or from senior management-level inputs.

A classic example of how forming a unique group based on sex, age, and specialty can improve existing research occurred when Fujitsu brought together a team of young female office workers, all fresh from college. They were given the task of designing a telephone especially for women. The result of their collaboration was even better than they had expected. In fact, their work caught the eye of the producers of the "Tonight Show" and Johnny Carson.

Because of its unique perspective, the group was able to think of features and characteristics that older male designers would never have considered. These features included an extremely lightweight and slim receiver that fits easily in a small hand. It is interesting to note that both men and women who repeatedly answered phones complimented the team on this aspect because it reduces the manual workout.

The female designers also changed the shape and colors so the phone could more easily fit in with an office worker's cramped, but often stylish, desk top. Also useful was a "knockout" feature that disconnects unwanted calls with a few harsh words in a strong male voice. This telephone has been extremely popular with Fujitsu's female customers. Even the telephone's name, "GooMog," would not have been easily thought of by male designers. *GooMog* is a shorthand phrase Japanese high school girls use when saying good morning to their close friends.

REVITALIZATION

At Fujitsu, it is common for experienced personnel to have positions on several research teams. This cross-application not only helps broaden training for new recruits but also helps prevent burnout by senior staff. Cross-application can help give any group a fresh outlook. The company notes that crossing fields of specialization has produced good results. For instance, researchers in communication have provided practical advice from a different angle to colleagues working on new-device technology.

Cross-application is only one way management tries to inject vigor into its mature organization. In fact, all areas within the organization are supposed to reassess their operation and to look at things in a new light and come up with new ideas on how to make it more effective and rewarding. Fujitsu's board of directors knew deeds speak louder than words, so it took the lead. It set up a blue-ribbon committee to evaluate its board's own way of doing business. To help ensure that the task force brought in a fresh perspective, the board decided that it would be chaired by the youngest section leader in its Corporate Planning Division and would be composed entirely of new employees, all with less than a few months' experience.

Asking fresh recruits to grade one's "old guard" is extremely unusual. Fujitsu believed that such recruits do not have any entrenched or ineffective ways of doing things and do not try to protect favorite projects. When the task force made its recommendations, most of the directors were both surprised and pleased by its findings. Many of the recommendations were implemented immediately, while some are expected to be implemented. Some recommendations could not be implemented until larger cultural changes could be made.

The point is that most of the board members did take the recommendations seriously. Naturally, not all of the task force's recommendations were well received by some of the board members; some even found the recommendations quite distasteful. After all, these are the normally conservative senior directors who typically lead companies. Takuma Yamanoto, chairman of the board, pointed out that they all had had their time to build the organization. He said the future of the organization belonged to its young people, all of whom would soon be in positions of authority and responsible for carrying on business.

CONCLUDING THOUGHTS

There is little doubt that Fujitsu knows how to carry out business; it is a world-class competitor. What made it so is a lesson well worth learning. It is a leading-edge, high-tech company that puts the emphasis where it should be—on its people.

A giant company like Fujitsu that is trying to keep empowered and maintain an entrepreneurial spirit presents challenges. It seems to be meeting the challenge of staying continuously competitive by focusing on streamlining and eliminating the bureaucracy that often chokes large organizations and by keeping the focus on the individual. It does this in part through its Ringi System, which reduces the bureaucracy and need for approvals. It also enhances its competitiveness through the use of subsidiaries that are given an arm's-length management approach.

The company has been able to apply three techniques to great advantage. Cross-cultural exchanges, cross-application of work, and intercultural teams have proven to b e strategic weapons that enhance innovativeness. Its recognition of the power of the individual is undoubtedly due to its success with individuals who "do great things." For this reason, it believes in a project director's total involvement with bringing a product to market. In this case, staff directs, and line follows the lead. Management follows, as much as it directs, R&D actions.

All of this flexibility in management gives Fujitsu enormous competitive muscle, but its receptiveness toward change marks it as a world-class competitor. It is always looking to the future, as evidenced by letting graduates fresh out of college grade its old guard and by listening to those suggestions. Maybe what really defines a competitive culture is that its members listen to each other and recognize that differences (different views, different experiences, different cultures) can be good.

11

Employee Involvement in a
Union Environment

In later chapters, we will look at a variety of innovative approaches to enhance both employee relations and productivity. While there may be more innovative approaches to employee relations and productivity, few experiences are more intriguing than the case of Ford Motor Company. It is the story of a highly autocratic organization that in the late 1970s was deep in financial trouble, yet turned its situation around to become the most successful of American automobile manufacturers.

This turnaround was in large measure due to some outstanding leadership and dramatic changes in the relationship between management and employees. It is a story of a cultural change that itself is remarkable. In the late 1970s Ford was a highly autocratic organization with traditional lines of authority. It also had an extremely aggressive union, the United Automobile Workers (UAW), which had an "us against them" temperament. Employee involvement (EI) has changed Ford's culture to one that is more participative, productive, and profitable. Today EI is a vital part of its culture and its enhanced relationship with its union. We will look at the background of EI and review the guidelines and ingredients for implementing it.

BACKGROUND

Originally, Ford Motor Company's EI efforts were not nearly as comprehensive nor as wide-ranging as they are today. In the early years, EI at Ford simply meant that groups of employees were getting together with their supervisors to identify and solve some work-related problems. While its initial efforts were to center around these problem-solving groups, Ford was eventually to go far beyond this level. First, though, let's look at how its EI efforts began.

Discussions between Ford's management and the UAW began in 1973, but real movement did not occur until their 1979 negotiations. In these union and management meetings, both sides discussed the benefits of greater participation in employee involvement efforts. They felt the benefits of EI included improved employee creativity, better relations, reduced absenteeism, and improved quality of their products (Savoie 1986).

Once Ford and the UAW jointly decided to pursue EI as an operational strategy, they decided they needed central coordination. To provide this, Ford and UAW leadership jointly provided a management-union initiative called the National Joint Committee on Employee Involvement (NJCEI). This organization was responsible for several activities, including reviewing and evaluating existing programs that were supposed to be improving the work environment. NJCEI was also charged with developing new projects and activities that encouraged employee participation and with reporting on the results of those activities.

COORDINATION AND SUPPORT

In terms of building employee involvement and relations, one of the most significant activities of NJCEI was to make a point of showing the rest of the corporation that EI had the support of the top management of both Ford and the UAW. NJCEI teams visited Ford plants to explain the principles of EI and provided guidelines for implementing it.

Among others, these NJCEI teams included union leaders and corporate labor relations representatives. As such, the composition of these teams clearly demonstrated the support by both management and labor.

Meetings conducted by these teams generally emphasized that EI efforts were separate from the normal collective bargaining agreements. EI was not to be thought of as a substitute for normal grievance procedures. Furthermore, the teams emphasized that participation in EI activities was purely voluntary and that any EI projects would be based on local needs—not corporate mandates. NJCEI teams told local facilities that, along with their efforts, locally elected union representatives were also to be directly involved in implementing any projects.

To continue to build support at the local level, NJCEI teams told these sites that EI efforts would slowly evolve rather than be forced on them. Finally, they made the point that local management and union leadership could terminate an EI project at any time. Once local EI projects were under way, the NJCEI would also make periodic visits to bolster morale and momentum.

Ford and UAW's efforts, through the NJCEI, to provide coordination and encouragement were not the only ways they communicated the importance of EI. Ford's CEO and other top officials also never failed to emphasize the importance of EI whenever they were at local facilities to make presentations to union leaders and other employees. They also used newsletters and brochures to drive home the same theme. The information presented through these forums revolved around the philosophy of EI, its benefits, the role of employees in this process, and general guidelines for implementing EI.

Another way Ford communicated the importance of EI was through two programs called the Mutual Growth Forum (MGF) and the Employee Development and Training Program (EDTP). The MGF was created in 1982 as a way to improve labor-management relations and two-way communications.

In general the purpose of MGF is for key members of management and the union to meet regularly to discuss issues of mutual concern. There is no formal collective bargaining at these forums, but almost any other subject is open to discussion. These discussions have included operating schedules, quality and performance indicators, product plans, new business opportunities, competition, economics, vacation scheduling, working conditions, attendance, and community government relations (Savoie 1986).

At the national level, MGF was used to create leadership conferences that brought together the top officials of both the company and the union. Open communication was an important aspect. Union leaders were briefed on the company's financial status and its competitors' new products and services. These conferences provide just one example of Ford's new attitude of greater sharing of information. The goal was greater acceptance and cooperation between the union and management, and it generally appears to be working.

EDTP

One indicator of the new shift in attitude can be seen in the joint UAW-Ford Employee Development and Training Program (EDTP). It was the first such case in which union and company management jointly developed training programs for both active and laid-off employees.

The EDTP created a national training center on the campus of the Henry Ford Community College in Dearborn, Michigan. The center was staffed by both union and management representatives as well as outside consultants. It is a brokering body, not a teaching entity. As much as possible, it uses programs offered through existing educational providers.

What makes EDTP unique in terms of employee involvement is that it has a Joint Governing Body that consists of representatives from the union and management. It and EDTP are funded by independently negotiated financial resources and managed by the Joint Governing Body. The educational activities at EDTP are based on participants' needs. To date, it has developed 17 major, distinct programs that were based on surveys of employees' needs and wants. EDTP has national educational programs, but each plant also has its own local EDTP committees and programs, which were locally initiated. Programs can be divided into those for either laid-off or active employees. Those for laid-off employees include:

- Education Fairs and Career Day Conferences
- Prepaid Tuition Assistance (the first in the country for laid-off employees)
- Job Search Skills Training
- Career Services and Reemployment Assistance Centers (nine of them provide comprehensive, one-stop placement and training services)
- Vocational Retraining (used to target occupations where jobs have been identified)
- Relocation Assistance Loans and Family Planning

Those programs for active employees include:

- Life/Education Planning Program (the first such program for blue-collar employees)
- A Tuition Assistance Plan (provides employees with wide latitude in selecting training and development courses)
- College and University Option Program (with on-site courses at Ford's plants)
- Targeted Education, Training, or Counseling Projects (which included training in computer literacy)
- A Basic Skills Enhancement Program (for such subjects as English and math)
- A Retirement Planning Program (for employees and spouses)

EDTP also provides funding support for local in-plant learning centers. The centers provide meeting room space, conference rooms, and audiovisual and technical equipment for all groups and employees involved in learning activities. The remarkable thing about these centers is that now hourly employees (who at one time were hired for narrowly defined tasks), along with management, have a place in the plant for problem solving and skill building (Savoie 1986).

Ford notes that EDTP, which training and retraining jointly sponsored by management and union, has had broad participation. In recent years, participation in its tuition assistance plan has tripled. Over 11,000 people have enrolled in its literacy courses, and more than 3,700 are in its basic skills programs delivered on site and in coordination with local school systems.

Perhaps because of the success of the joint labor and management approach, in 1984 EDTP, Ford, and the UAW also restructured their Employee Assistance Plan (EAP) so it would be a joint initiative. It is designed to help employees change their life-styles to improve their general health and well-being. It is entirely voluntary and is designed to assist employees who may have alcohol, drug dependency, health, or other serious personal problems. EAP also provides a referral system for professional evaluation, counseling, and treatment. Also included are wellness programs that include health risk appraisals, smoking cessation, hypertension screening, stress management, and nutrition and exercise programs.

All of Ford's employee involvement (EI) initiatives can be distilled to four broad principles. Ford's EI efforts seek to involve its work force and union in both the work to be done and the operation of the business. Key initiatives have included specific EI activities, which we will discuss, and its Mutual Growth Forum. Second, it tried to show it cared about the total welfare of the employee in the workplace and beyond. Initiatives have included its EDTP and EAP as well as Child Care Projects. Third, Ford's EI efforts focused on recognizing the contributions of employees. Finally, it rewarded its work force with job security and a good benefits and compensation package as well as a profit-sharing program (Savoie 1986). Out of this process came guidelines that could help anyone who is considering implementing EI activities.

GUIDELINES

Ford's guidelines for effective EI consist of eight steps. The first step involved developing union and management support. Ford was able to build an image of support through its joint decision making on EI matters. This support came primarily through the NJCEI. It also publicized its corporate- and union-supported *Letter of Understanding*, which described EI efforts and, along with other policy letters and visits by NJCEI, helped reinforce the impression that EI was a joint effort between labor and management.

Another method was to encourage local area personnel who were thinking of implementing EI to visit plants and peers where it had been implemented. This brings up a key point. Although EI efforts had joint upper management and labor support, Ford wisely knew local ownership was needed. For this reason Ford and UAW management decided whether or not EI was implemented at specific sites should be left to the local people, who were the ones who would have to implement it.

This second step, assuming a local site wanted to implement EI, involved setting up a joint steering committee. This committee at the local level was charged with setting objectives, diagnosis, developing local guidelines for implementing EI, assigning responsibilities, communicating, and resolving other EI-related problems (Banas 1988).

Ford felt its most effective steering committees consisted of three or four members. Membership of these committees should consist of members of the local union bargaining committee, as well as representatives of management. It also discovered that it is better when senior management and a union person on the committee jointly serve as cochairs. Ford also pointed out that with all the expectations put on the committee, it was wise for someone to be employed as a full-time involvement coordinator, who at Ford was usually a staff individual.

Ford's third step was its actual diagnosis by the steering committee. This stage consisted of gathering information about local work relationships to determine if an area was ready for EI activities. Also included in this third stage was identifying factors that would help achieve EI objectives.

The fourth step in the process was selecting a pilot site. Each steering committee at a local site would look for a location or area where the union, employees, and supervisors were receptive to participating in a pilot project. Setting up a pilot project in a relatively stable environment where supervisors and employees were stable was also another important variable. Ford favored pilot sites that were primarily self-contained units, rather than one section of a larger unit. Such areas included work areas where employees produced an identifiable product and involved the work of only a simple work group.

Preparation of the organization was the fifth step. Naturally, as with anything new, there will be misconceptions about EI. Some supervisors will think it is a way of undermining their authority or even see it as a way of getting rid of them. Some employees and unions may think EI activities will undermine their grievance procedures. Still others will think it is management's way of speeding up the production or as a way to eliminate jobs.

To dispel these misconceptions, Ford used letters from the joint steering committee, informational meetings, brochures, bulletin boards, and special visits by NJCEI. The steering committee's job was to determine what was needed to dispel these misconceptions and what kind of education and training was needed to implement EI.

The sixth step was actually initiating a pilot project. Again, it was the steering committee's primary responsibility to select a pilot area, provide guidelines, and oversee and train participants. The committee also provided a direction for the process, a place to meet, access to resources, and monitoring of results.

The seventh step in Ford's EI process involved evaluation. As already noted, although Ford did not evaluate its problem-solving or quality circle team's performance, it did want to know several things about the overall EI process. It needed some feedback on what was working and not working and needed to know whether or not its efforts were achieving its goals. If not, then it could decide what should be done differently.

To help answer these questions, Ford relied on four activities. It evaluated a local site's EI efforts by judging the quality of the recommendations made to the steering committee. The committee also sought feedback and opinions of its problem-solving groups and evaluated the quality of its EI education and training at a site. Finally, the committee looked at expansion of EI activities at specific sites.

While these four variables were quantifiable measures, no specific, formal, quantitative measurements were used. Ford apparently felt it was important for the numbers not to be more important than establishing a viable EI process. It was a time to establish trust, not set standards. Regardless of the reason, lack of measurement made it easier for people to experiment with EI activities, because it helped eliminate an element of fear.

The last stage of Ford's EI process would be expected to be a natural part to any EI efforts. If the previous stages are properly implemented, then EI pilot projects should be expected to lead to increases in the number and scope of problem-solving groups and other related activities. At least that is the way Ford sees it, and it has created a variety of EI related teams to help expand those efforts.

As part of this expansion process, Ford makes use of "interface groups." These groups are formed whenever an EI problem is discovered that cuts across work groups. Sometimes Ford also finds it necessary to make use of "opportunity teams." These teams are formed whenever work-related changes provide an opportunity to use EI, for example, when the company plans to introduce new products, make changes in its facilities, and so on. Opportunity teams are only one of a long line of teams Ford uses to spread the influence of EI.

"Special project teams" are similar to opportunity teams except that they are formed around an event that is typically larger than that usually handled by the normal problem-solving groups. Such activities might include a particular location's participation in an auto show and visits by an NJCEI team. When the event is over, the team is disbanded.

"Linking teams" are groups whose members come from several other teams and whose purpose is interdepartmental. "Launch teams" participate in the final stages of product and process development; the launch team's primary purpose is coordination with other groups that are involved. Ford also uses its team approach when working with outside organizations. Teams are formed whose purpose is to meet with vendor representatives or with groups of employees in its other plants or other companies. Discussion subjects in these teams usually revolve around how to improve communication and prevent future problems.

WHAT WAS LEARNED

There are several things we can learn from Ford's experience. First, a great deal of its success is due to the fact that it established a local as well as corporate structure to promote and encourage EI activities.

Second, success depends on good communication. Between 1979 and 1976, the NJCEI sent out 26 newsletters reviewing various aspects of employee involvement. There was information on NJCEI's own role structure and membership. Newsletters also discussed guidelines for implementing EI and provided information on the role of its local joint steering committees. Other newsletters discussed seminars and workshops that were available. Ford also sent other letters, pamphlets, booklets, handbooks, and even reference guides for implementing EI.

All of these activities were supplemented by local communication. In addition to this corporate NJCEI, local plants also did an effective job at communicating. Many local plants held "state-of-the-plant" meetings. These plants also supplemented corporate communication by using local management and union newspapers to describe the EI achievement at their sites. Of course, there were also numerous speeches made by both union and management representatives at conferences, workshops, and national conventions.

THE ROLE OF EDUCATION

Another key ingredient in Ford's EI success was its extensive educational and training efforts. The heart of these efforts was a series of workshops, one of which was called the Joint UAW-Ford Employee Involvement Process Workshop. This particular workshop was developed for employee involvement coordinators (salaried) and facilitators (hourly). Training included giving them an understanding of the eight-step guidelines and reviewing how to diagnose problems, management styles, group dynamics, and other aspects of communication.

Some of Ford's other popular workshops focused on creative problem solving and instructional skills. These instructional skills workshops helped facilitators and coordinators upgrade their instructional skills. Other workshops covered related EI aspects, including how to prepare managers and supervisors on their responsibilities for implementing EI.

In addition to these workshops, Ford also used conferences as a means of sharing EI experiences. Normally these meetings included keynote speeches by union leaders and company executives. There were also talks by experts of EI subjects as well as experimental and informational sharing sessions. Other resources to communicate and educate included committees that evaluated competencies.

All of this communication, instructional support, and support of top officials in both the union and management did pay off. Not only did Ford become more competitive, but employee attitudes and relations with management improved substantially. A survey of employees showed overwhelming support for EI efforts and some nice extras. In a survey, 2,000 people were asked whether they agreed with the statement "All in all, I am satisfied with my job." Before EI efforts, 58 percent of participants agreed with this statement. After it was in operation, those agreeing with the statement rose to 82 percent (Banas 1988). Even nonparticipants in the EI process changed their opinion of their work environment: before EI, 67 percent agreed with the above statement; after EI, the figure rose to 75 percent. The bottom line is that EI enhanced employee relations and employee satisfaction with their jobs.

All in all, EI has been a positive experience for Ford, but any journey as grand as this is bound to have a few bumps. Initially, Ford's efforts revolved around problem-solving groups. These groups would then get together with supervisors to identify and solve work-related problems. These initial attempts were not as successful as it hoped, and it found it needed to redefine its concept of employee involvement.

When Ford began introducing employee involvement at its plants, it focused on educating and training hourly employees. This focus was good, except that it initially did not pay that much attention to those supervisors and managers who were critical to the success of EI efforts. Ford did orient these managers to EI and did encourage them to practice it, but it did not make clear exactly what participative management meant and its relationship to employee involvement. It felt it was important for these people to understand the theory behind the technique.

DEFINING PM AND EI

To correct this deficiency, Ford created a model to explain the relationship of participative management (PM) to its EI efforts. Ford explained that PM consisted of techniques and skills managers used to provide employees with an opportunity to participate in managerial processes like planning, goal setting, problem solving, and decision making affecting job-related activities (Banas 1988).

Examples of the managerial skills needed by those wishing to practice PM include contracting, which involves discussions that establish the expectations that group members, including the managers, have for one another and the group. The second skill needed is the ability to reward or give positive feedback to individuals and groups. The third skill Ford believes essential to practice PM it calls modeling, so others may learn to perform by imitation.

From the EI standpoint, there is a range of opportunities to participate. Ford defines these as consultation, collaboration, or delegation. A manager who practices a consultative approach simply requests information and opinion from employees. The advantage of this approach is that the manager gains the benefit of finding out what employees are thinking. This approach requires that the manager spend time selling the idea to employees to ensure understanding and commitment, since employees probably will have limited commitment.

Greater employee commitment comes through a collaborative process, in which a manager solicits employee input, exchanges information, and discusses employee concerns. The group tries for a "win-win" approach where no one feels like a loser. If this approach is achieved, the outcome has everyone's support because consensus is the norm.

The last PM approach a Ford manager can choose is a delegative process where a manager outlines the constraints or standards needed. Responsibility for that outcome is assigned to the group, and the manager goes on to other activities (Banas 1984).

Ford became famous for repeatedly making the point that PM and EI are simply two sides of the same coin. This relationship is seen in Figure 11.1. The point is that you cannot have one without the other. PM, as viewed from the manager's perspective, occurs when a manager tries to involve employees in the decision-making process and tries to obtain employee opinions and get them to participate in problem solving.

ACCEPTANCE

Many of the bumps Ford experienced were due to initial lack of acceptance of EI by local managers and union people. One of the primary ways Ford was able to overcome this obstacle was to encourage skeptics to visit plants that had succeeded at implementing some aspects of EI. This opportunity to talk to peers seemed to be of the greatest value in expanding employee involvement throughout the corporation. Another factor contributing to Ford's success and acceptance of EI was its emphasis on pilot projects. The knowledge and understanding gained here were effectively used to implement EI throughout the corporation. Acquiring this initial understanding of how to implement EI is the most difficult part of the process. Once this ignorance is breached, the speed of implementing EI is multiplied throughout the organization.

All too often, upper management believes all it needs to implement a directive is to tell someone about it. Many EI efforts, like the quality of work life and quality circles, have risen and fallen in popularity. The fault is not the approach; rather it lies in how it was implemented. If

Figure 11.1
Ford's Model for PM/EI

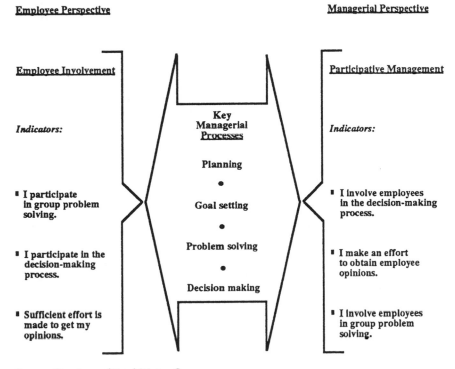

Source: Courtesy of Ford Motor Company

management feels EI is something it must tell to lower managers, then it is doomed to failure. For this reason most EI efforts do not sustain themselves. This "I tell, you do" attitude must be overcome if EI is to last. Paul Banas, who was then in charge of Ford's human resource efforts, says everyone must have the opportunity to participate (Savoie 1986). All levels and all employees, not just top managers, must have the opportunity to participate. Only when we participate do we appreciate.

CHAMPIONS

Ever notice that unfortunately it almost always takes a crisis before things change? There is a great force that keeps things static and at the status quo. The same is true when trying to change organizations. To implement EI, a company needs either a crisis or a champion. Ever since the competition with the Japanese and the rest of the world, U.S. management has grudgingly begun to change the way it conducts business.

Only when there is a tight labor market or an increasing need for better-trained employees do we change. Few would be discussing EI unless there were problems in the status quo. Only when a crisis occurs is EI perceived as a possible solution. In times of a crisis, champions must emerge. Banas says that if there is no crisis, the human resource people must become these champions (Savoie 1986).

Champions are needed because while the rewards are great, there is a cost. EI takes investment of money, time, facilities, and people and requires training and education. For this reason Ford recommends EI aspirations be part of the labor contract. In the 1980s Ford was in financial trouble, but despite extensive cost cutting, EI needs remained paramount. Banas feels that such "sacred" attitudes toward EI monies are essential for long-term, sustained effort.

CONCLUDING THOUGHTS

To implement EI and reap the benefits of improved relations and productivity, an organization's decision-making process must change. Decision making must be less authoritarian, more focused on participation, less focused on management and more focused on employees.

Not only must the focus change, but local or plant-level people must "buy into" the process. It means local ownership and, most importantly, local control. Corporate management cannot simply tell local sites what to do and expect it to get done. There must be significant local involvement. There must be local control over objectives, methods, resources, communication, and even evaluation of the success of the process.

The need for local control does not imply that there are no corporate guidelines. At Ford, guidelines for EI were hammered out between its top management and the top leadership of its union. Guidelines and encouragement must come from the top, but local leaders must decide when they are ready for EI and how to do it.

Because of this rationale, NJCEI did not set corporatewide, specific criteria for measuring the effectiveness of local EI efforts. It felt systematic, corporatewide attempts to measure the effectiveness of EI efforts would make the "numbers" more important than the process. In fact, the surveys of employees' opinions about the value of their EI process were the only evidence of EI's effect on Ford.

Another key point to remember is that EI is not self-generating. It will not continue without champions. There must continue to be adequate resources, education, training, and recognition of EI efforts if it is to be sustained.

Banas emphasized, though, that the main obstacles to implementing EI are political. Politics delayed EI's implementation when one of the candidates for a bargaining chair made a point of strongly opposing EI;

as fate would have it, this candidate won. Although it was a setback, it was only a temporary one. It was NJCEI's job to assess these situations and help change them.

In some cases personality can also come into play. Personality clashes more than once have inhibited EI efforts. Managers and/or union leaders at specific sites can have conflicts with each other due to different operational philosophies. Some managers prefer more autocratic management styles. Ford dealt with this issue by making sure managers knew their actions toward EI would be part of their performance evaluation.

In some cases, you can expect all talk and no action. There is lip service and little else. In some cases, expect outright resistance. To help solve this, EI at Ford was part of its labor contract and part of its company policy. It also discussed cooperative and resistive behaviors as part of each person's performance evaluation.

Ford has joint steering committees at its various sites and 175 coordinators and facilitators. More than 1,200 employees have attended its Employee Involvement Process Workshops. More than 10,000 managers and supervisors have received training in participative management (Savoie 1986). More than half of the company's employees have received some EI-related orientation and training. Ford continues to broaden the communication and information sharing between management and labor. Team management has increased.

All of this activity has resulted in rearrangement of production lines, elimination of scrap and rework, and improved cooperation with suppliers. During this period, product quality improved 50 percent for Ford's cars and 47 percent for its trucks (Savoie 1986). In succeeding chapters, we will look more specifically at EI techniques and how to enhance employee relations and corporate productivity.

REFERENCES

Banas, Paul A. *The Relationship Between Participative Management and Employee Involvement at Ford Motor Company* (in-house publication), May 16, 1984, 1–2.

Banas, Paul A. "Employee Involvement: A Sustained Labor/Management Initiative at the Ford Motor Company." In John P. Campbell and Richard J. Campbell, *Productivity in Organizations New Perspectives from Industrial and Organizational Psychology.* San Francisco: Jossey-Bass, 1988.

Savoie, Ernest J. *Creating the Work Force of the Future: The Ford Focus* (in-house publication), September 16, 1986, 6.

12

Management Through
Multiskilled Teams

In discussing the problems of productivity, Peter Drucker described a "double-breasted" contractor who had both a union and a nonunion crew working on a job. The nonunion crew worked an average of 50 minutes out of every hour, while the union crew worked only 35 minutes (Drucker 1988). Drucker also noted that the same job required eight employees from the union crew, but only five employees from a nonunion crew.

Drucker was not criticizing unions as much as he was criticizing the way unions dichotomize work and the corresponding effect on productivity. He described the U.S. Honda or Toyota facility, which has only three to five job classifications. A corresponding General Motors, Ford, or Chrysler plant of comparable size has almost 60 job classifications.

This dichotomization and proliferation of work restrictions and job classification are seen by many management experts as a serious challenge to our ability to remain competitive. But things are starting to change. Ford, for instance, has joint union-management efforts under way to increase productivity by reducing job classifications in one of its larger plants (Drucker 1988).

MULTISKILLING

Overspecialization of job duties is the enemy of productivity. At some point specialization may have been necessary, but today it has hampered what people can do. It has often led to feelings of alienation by many of the work force since employees and managers feel they are only a cog in the organizational machinery.

One of the solutions to the problem of specialization is called multi-skilling. Some call it cross training. Regardless of what you call it, its aim remains the same: improve productivity and quality by developing a broader, more flexible work force. It is having an effect. Union companies like G.M. and National Steel have improved speed and efficiencies by losing job classifications. Motorola trained workers how to do several jobs and solved critical quality problems with its cellular phone (Alster 1990).

Multiskilling usually involves being paid for the variety of skills one masters rather than for the job one has acquired. John F. Krafcik, consultant to MIT's International Motor Vehicle program, emphasized the significance of multiskilling when he said that around the world there is a very strong correlation in durable goods manufacturing and quality and productivity, and the use of multiskilling, worker teams, and just-in-time (Alster 1990). As an example, Motorola had a quality problem and used multiskilling as part of its solution.

Motorola needed to reduce the defects in manufacturing its cellular telephones and so shifted responsibility to line workers and overhauled its compensation system. True to the nature of multiskilling, Motorola rewarded those who learned a variety of skills, and its defect rate fell by 77 percent (Alster 1990). At its Arlington Heights, Illinois, cellular phone factory, it also got rid of six pay categories. Now all workers are in the same category. Employees get pay increases provided they learn new skills and maintain their quality at their workstation at zero defects for five consecutive days.

Multiskilling not only holds great promise for making companies more competitive but also creates greater employee flexibility and enhanced employee performance and relations. Lechmere, Inc., a 27-store retail chain, offers proof of this point. At its Sarasota, Florida, outlet, raises are based on the number of jobs its people learn (Alster 1990). Cashiers are also encouraged to sell products; sporting goods people receive training in how to operate forklifts. As a result of this and other multiskilling training, it is able to adjust staffing needs by rerouting employees. One of the results is a more stable work force. The company also notes that pay incentives, along with the prospect of a more varied and interesting work day, proved valuable lures in recruiting (Alster 1990). Finally, it points out that its Sarasota store has 60 percent full-timers versus the average 30 percent for the rest of its chain. As might be expected, the store is also more productive.

PRODUCT DEVELOPMENT TEAMS

Multiskilling is itself a powerful tool, but it can be greatly enhanced when used within a team concept. AT&T is applying the concept of multi-department teams to product development. It gives its teams tough deadlines and authority, and they are producing results. It used to take two years to design a new telephone, but the company realized that if it could get its product to the market sooner, it would have a strategic advantage.

In 1988, AT&T began developing a new cordless phone but faced a rigid internal bureaucracy. John Hanley, AT&T's vice president of product development, wanted to cut 50 percent off development time, but he knew they would have to make some dynamic changes. In the past, AT&T's product development resembled a relay system that involved handing a design over to manufacturing, which in turn handed the finished product to marketing to sell (Dumaine 1989).

His solution was to form 6 to 12 teams that included engineers, manufacturers, and marketers. They were given the authority to make every decision on how the product would work, look, be made, and cost. The key was to set rigid speed requirements before freezing design requirements. Since the teams did not need to send decisions up the line for approval, they were able to meet their tight deadlines. As a result of its new team approach, AT&T was able to cut development time from two years to just one year. A bonus was lower cost and improved quality.

Some companies are even using suppliers as part of their team approach. Navistar, a Chicago truck maker, had a major contract with U-Haul. It wanted to make the truck bed 24 inches off the ground, compared with the normal 48 inches. The truck required a new chassis design and a new suspension system. To enhance the speed of the projects, the company used a team approach where suppliers were a vital part of that team. The team succeeded in large part because of supplier involvement. Teams continue to become an even more integral part of day-to-day management.

WORK DESIGN TEAMS

One company that has had extensive experience with both multiskilling and team management is Hoechst Celanese Corporation. The company is both innovative and diversified. Its Salisbury, North Carolina, plant is one of its locations that is using multiskilled teams to enhance performance and competitiveness.

The plant's decision making is extraordinary. For instance, when three employees of a 32-person work unit at the Salisbury fiber plant left, a decision was made not to replace them. While at first this may not seem extraordinary, it was. It was not management that decided not to replace them; rather, the employee members of the work unit did not replace them. Most would consider such staffing decisions to be the domain of management, but it was work unit employees who made the decision.

Dave Henderson, one of the operators in the work unit, said, "Even though we were told we could replace them, we decided we could handle the work load by reassigning crew schedules" (Stine 1989, 7). This was not the first decision the work unit members made. Three years earlier the same group decided it could operate with seven fewer people, including one supervisor.

Team managerial decision making is not unusual at the 2,000-employee plant. One particularly effective team decision-making approach for the Hoechst Celanese plant is something it calls "work design teams." In this process, teams of employees are selected from a specific work area to look at both internal and external factors affecting their jobs. In analyzing those factors affecting their jobs, teams consider productivity, quality, safety, and customer service as well as their own employee satisfaction. Ultimately, the objective is for employees to participate and assume greater job responsibilities.

At the Salisbury plant, participation in team decision making is not a small pilot or experiment. More than 70 percent of the plant production employees have been involved in this process, and they are effective. Plant Manager Carl Repsher says teams have reduced cost by at least $8 million annually through productivity improvements (Stine 1989).

Repsher says that because of these teams, employees are more committed. Employees do not simply come to work and do what someone tells them to do. Instead, because of these teams, employees have a sense of ownership. The same sentiment was expressed by Ron Holt, a computer mechanic, who said: "It's the best thing the company has done in the last ten years. You know your ideas are accepted and you mean something to the total operation" (Stine 1989, 8).

According to Work Design Superintendent Rip Kersey, the reason the company uses these teams is that it wants high-quality decisions as well as acceptance on the floor. Work design teams fit that bill. Typically, operators decide on such things as vacation and work scheduling. They also review requests for appropriations, seek peer performance review, and provide input or correction action needed.

The work design concept was first introduced at Salisbury in 1984. The initial goal was to improve work assignments for a major new piece of technology the company was introducing. A team of operators and supervisors studied the problem of the new equipment and then reorganized the work area. Over a three-year period they continued to make recommendations, including eliminating three supervisors and eight operators through attrition.

Gradually, the team assumed more supervisory responsibility. Currently, there is only one supervisor for the 20 operators in the area. This process has evolved to the point that the area is now a self-managed work environment. There are no supervisors present during the night shift, and delegates chosen by these employees perform normal administrative talks and resolve social issues. If a problem that the group is unable to handle does occur, it can reach its supervisor by beeper. Usually these calls have been limited to major maintenance problems.

Beyond those initial efforts, work design teams have been used to cut costs and improve productivity. In 1986, when an economic downturn occurred in the industry, work design teams, which included both operators and supervisors, recommended staffing cuts, cost-saving measures, and quality improvements. One hundred jobs were also eliminated through attrition and voluntary separation. Kersey said that initially operators feared work design would eliminate their jobs. When they saw the company was committed to avoiding furloughs unless through attrition or special separation packages, they felt much better about the process.

ENVIRONMENTAL SCAN

Hoechst Celanese's work design efforts begin with an environmental scan. This involves human resource people teaching employees about import trends, cost pressures, and the products market outlook. The company also makes a point of examining how communication and work relationships in an area can be improved and how to make employees' jobs more interesting. This goal usually involves assigning greater responsibility and accountability. To help employees handle this greater responsibility and accountability, team members undergo multiskill training in such areas as problem solving and conflict resolution. The skills of these team members are also enhanced by letting them have greater access to more information about their operations. Plant Manager Repsher says the objective of this information-sharing process is to get across an impression of the big picture that is occurring, for example, through state-of-the-plant presentations given twice a year.

With enhanced problem-solving skills and more open access to corporate information, team members gather the information needed to develop work design recommendations. A plant steering committee normally accepts these recommendations, assuming they fall within the normal parameters of plant policies, length of service, quality, and safety considerations.

Work design team members are selected by their peers, according to how much they know about all the jobs in the area. They meet regularly and obtain feedback from fellow employees on proposals they make. The perspective is managerial as well as employee. Dave Henderson, a unit operator sitting on a work design team that had been in operation for a year, said, "Once a week we [unit and work design team] meet to determine where we're making money and where we're losing it" (Stine

1989, 10). It should be noted that since the use of the work design team, the unit turned an interval profit for the first time in 14 years.

CREATING A TEAM PERSPECTIVE

Work design teams are a vital part of Hoechst Celanese Corporation's Salisbury plant, but they certainly are not the only way it creates a self-managed perspective. At the plant, employees choose (among themselves) a coordinator. This person starts work earlier than the rest of them and makes sure there is a smooth transition from one shift to another. The position is rotated among group members so eventually everyone gets a chance to be the coordinator.

In line with the true nature of multiskilled teams, the Salisbury plant also has self-managed groups in its utilities areas. These teams get involved in all facets of decision making. A key to their effectiveness is that they are organized by equipment rather than by skill. This way employees are familiar with all jobs related to that equipment and fill in for each other at any time (Stine 1989). The night shift of this maintenance group does not even have a supervisor available, so it keeps in constant communication through hand-held walkie-talkies.

Multiskilled teams are not limited to Hoechst Celanese Corporation's Salisbury plant. At its Chemical Groups plant in Clear Lake, Texas, it has made extensive use of multiskilled teams. It was here that management asked 129 craftspeople and foremen to create a new maintenance organization. Reorganization of the maintenance area was not easy or quick, but it had many positive benefits. Larry Butz, an electrician in the area, said the way the company went about reorganizing made him feel more like a decision maker and that he loves the additional responsibility and takes pride in his contribution (Alinsworth 1989). Under their reorganization, craftspeople have more day-to-day managerial responsibilities, including planning routine jobs, screening job applicants, and determining the distribution of crafts in each production area.

When plant management first decided to reorganize, it felt it was essential that the reorganization be compatible with Hoechst Celanese's values. With this guide, the maintenance reorganization attempted to involve more people in decision making at the lowest level, as well as enhance customer service and focus on continual improvement. As the first step, committees consisting of seven managers, 129 craftspeople and supervisors, and 24 maintenance engineers and planners developed a mission statement. It read, "As part of the plant team, we maintain and improve plant facilities and provide quality service in a safe and efficient manner" (Alinsworth 1989, 16).

Once the mission statement was developed, management held additional meetings with its craftspeople and, as a result of these meetings, agreed to decentralize the maintenance organization, with teams of craftspeople and foremen in each unit. Craftspeople decided who among the group would do what by having their members sign up for jobs on a large board.

As a result of this activity, over 90 percent of the craftspeople ended up with jobs they wanted. Contrary to what one might first think, there was very little fighting over the same slots. They were able to compromise. The process of reorganization took nine months instead of the one month it would have taken if just a few managers had been involved. Both parties agreed the longer route was better (Alinsworth 1989).

Today there is greater sense of ownership, as evidenced by the comments of Butz. He said that in the past if the lighting in an area was poor, craftspeople did not know who was responsible for it because they were in and out of an area many times. Now, since they are in the same area every day, they make sure the lights work in their area. Maintenance employees also say they now have greater responsibility to monitor equipment and trouble spots.

To enhance maintenance responsibilities and accountabilities, craftspeople decided to redo the way jobs were handled. In the past when maintenance work was needed, a production unit would write a request for service (RFS) and send it to a planner. The planner in turn sent it to a scheduler, who then sent it to a craftsperson. One individual noted that it often took longer to go through this process than to do the job. Now, after reorganization, foremen bypass RFS by writing out requests for small jobs without involving the planners and schedulers. They do this by simply placing the request in a box outside their offices so craftspeople can move to another job as soon as they are free.

MULTISKILLED TEAMS

While the case of Hoechst Celanese's Clear Lake, Texas, plant involved only reorganizing maintenance into areas, the corporation's Celeo plant in Narrow, Virginia, makes even broader use of multiskilling. This plant consists of several operations, but its nine-member production group that manufactures a new cellulose acetate product is of most interest. Sam McNair, supervisor of the group, says he thinks of himself as a supervisor without subordinates. This team is unusual because everyone on the team is a decision maker and everyone is a generalist (O'Connell 1990). Everyone can do everyone else's job.

To understand this process we need to look at what the plant was trying to achieve and how this generalist team came about. The plant employs 1,800 people and tries to foster independent action. To this end, there are no area superintendents, no shift supervisors, no one between the operators and McNair, who is a senior development engineer.

In forming the initial team, the plant posted five generalist jobs, and over 100 employees bid for them. The final hiring decision was based on seniority. Before this stage, candidates were narrowed down based on past performance, attendance records, and aptitude tests. Management was looking for people who were flexible, reliable, and able to learn.

Management felt learning was essential because each person would have to be a generalist, not a specialist. Members of the team had to operators; if something broke, they had to be repair persons. They had to be problem solvers if anything, including procedures, were in doubt. If their product needed analysis, then they had to be lab technicians. When members of the team were chosen, they went through 90 days of "intense" training.

The team of five was eventually increased to nine. These nine operate and maintain the department 24 hours a day. McNair's hours overlap two of the four shifts, but he is not there most of the time, and never on weekends. Only when something extraordinary occurs does the team need to contact McNair.

Ellis Martin, an operator/mechanics on the team, echoes the feelings of most of the team when he says the best part of his job is making his own decisions. He says you learn to trust the person who knows more about something than you do. Another operator/mechanic, Fred Thompson, says, "We'll ask each other, and listen, and learn" (O'Connell 1990, 9). He says that learning something on the job makes it more enjoyable. Since the project started, Thompson has taken related courses like Organizational Behavior and Change and hands-on courses on machine-shop practice.

TEAMS, TEAMS, TEAMS

One final example of Hoechst Celanese Corporation's extensive use of teams comes from its plant in Rock Hill, South Carolina. Here you can see the power of multiskilled teams as they interact with each other. The plant has a process it calls Total Employee Involvement (TEI).

TEI involves forming department teams and then getting members of the teams involved in making decisions and solving problems for the department. Typical decisions involve setting goals, analyzing product quality, and scheduling work. One of these departments, called Beaming Department, formed its own team in 1987. A related department, called the Extrusion Department, was formed in 1989. The relationship between these two departments shows the true power of teams.

The Extrusion Department was the natural internal customer for the

Beaming Department. In an innovation, these two teams formed an internal customer-supplier agreement that spells out product specifications and quality standards. Both department teams meet regularly to see how well they are meeting the terms of their agreement.

It is a better arrangement for all concerned. One extrusion operator noted that in the past, she never thought of the Beaming Department's problems as affecting her department. With both TEI groups, she has a different opinion. The groups feel their one-on-one meetings between operators in both departments have gone a long way toward resolving past misunderstandings and problems. As a result, the Beaming Department has decreased its quality alerts by 75 percent (Braun 1990). (A quality alert occurs when a nonconforming product leaves a department and needs recalling.) In addition, the Beaming Department's productivity has risen 45 percent.

Like the previous examples, TEI groups are an example of multiskilling because they are organized around what they call ownership of machines. Essentially, this means an operator is responsible for all aspects of keeping machines running, including start-up, shutdown, identifying malfunctions, taking care of breaks, and other related problems. A unit supervisor, Bill Batson, says operators are running their own business and explains that supervisors are more like coaches and resource people (Braun 1990).

CREATING A SENSE OF TEAMWORK

Teams can be an effective way to improve productivity, employee relations, and motivation. The secret is to be able to create a sense of ownership and a sense of teamwork within the team. Obviously, Hoechst Celanese Corporation's many successes with its teams have shown, at least in some cases, that it was able to create teamwork.

Another case is from the giant General Electric (G.E.) Corporation. At G.E.'s facility in Decatur, Alabama, there is no shortage of teams to help build its refrigerators. At the plant, employees are divided into teams according to location or type of work. Each team acts as a separate business, making sure that its piece of the job is the very best it can be (Dwyer 1990).

One example of these teams is called the Alpha Specialist, which is a team of eight people who work together at the start of the main assembly line. Team leader Charlie Wilson says that they used to come to work, leave their brains at the door, put in their hours, and get their paycheck. Now everyone cares more, because the work force is self-directed. According to Plant Manager Dave Caplinger, teamwork requires that you, as a team member, keep learning.

It is not only team members who must constantly be learning and changing. Under this new system, supervisors' roles also change. Naturally, some supervisors do not like the change, because they do not want to give up the power, their ties, or their authoritarian styles, which can be symbols of their having made it. There are no easy answers to such a situation; many of these people will have to be reeducated.

While some supervisors resist the change to team management, others welcome it. Jim Ernest is one supervisor at G.E. who likes it. He is a business team leader of the main assembly line, where some 90 people are divided into teams to assemble refrigerators. He said he used to be a hands-on supervisor with day-to-day worries. Now, rather than telling the team what to do and acting as a watchdog (Dwyer 1990), he does more looking ahead and planning and guiding the team. Mary Rutherford, an employee on the team, says: "It's quicker and easier to get things done. We rotate jobs so that everyone on the team knows all the jobs" (Dwyer 1990, 16). She says that sometimes working together as a team can be aggravating, but they all know it is necessary and, in the long run, good for everyone.

How do you create the sense of teamwork so essential to harmony and team success? At G.E., before people are hired, they attend prehire classes that run three hours a day, two days a week. In these meetings they talk about competition, quality, and productivity. Management tries to make sure everyone knows what he or she is getting into. It is a matter of constant communication and team-building exercises.

One interesting team-building exercise was explained by Rutherford. It involves having employees set up an assembly line for making paper airplanes. Each person is to make a fold and pass on the paper. People cannot talk to each other. At the end of the line, the planes are flight-tested. She says, as you can imagine, many planes do not fly. Next, they do the same exercise, except this time they can talk to each other. The planes fly. The exercise makes the point that teamwork is essential in success.

Another way G.E. creates a sense of teamwork is through the sharing of information. One such example involves birthdays. Twice a day, two or three times a week, about a dozen people whose birthdays fall in that month join Plant Manager Caplinger for a roundtable discussion about the state of the plant, its business, and the competition. It is a casual get-together that makes the information sharing even more effective.

SELF-REGULATING TEAMS

One of the most comprehensive approaches to team management involves a small plant in La Porte, Texas. All 67 employees at the plant are actively involved in decision making, including evaluating the performance of coworkers, hiring new employees, and even disciplining employees whose behavior they consider unacceptable. The plant is a subsidiary of Rohm and Haas Company, and its plant manager is Robert D. Gilbert.

He believes that too much hierarchy is one of the causes of poor productivity, so one of the first things he wanted to do was to try to run the facility without shift foremen. Eventually, he went a step further by eliminating the position of general foreman.

Gilbert said he wanted to create a workplace where people could be both responsible for their own work and involved in managing their own work (Dumaine 1989). To accomplish this goal, the plant's personnel developed outcome statements about what they wanted the plant to be, by talking with their middle managers, employees, and corporate personnel. It took them about three months to come up with six outcome statements, which focused on such things as the plant being customer-focused, people-oriented, cost-effective, multiskilled, and so on.

They felt that a traditional hierarchy would not reflect the kind of philosophy outlined in their outcome statements; therefore, they developed a "focused-factory" approach. Eventually, they came up with three functional teams (Bayport Diphenyl [BDP], Bayport Specialty Monomer [BSM], and their administrative team [office technicians, and so on]) connected to each other by a management team, which consists of Gilbert, their financial analyst, a personal manager, and their two manufacturing managers.

At the facility, task force teams are formed as needed to solve particular problems. These teams include all groups and levels of supervision. For instance, such a team could be formed to work on the problems of drug abuse policy, to deal with their performance evaluation system, and to help them evaluate the feasibility of 12-hour shifts rather than 8-hour shifts.

The plant also functions with the four teams of technicians (two for each operation). Each team either works the day or night shift. The day shift goes from 7 A.M. to 7 P.M., four days a week; the night shift goes from 7 P.M. to 7 A.M., four nights a week. They are essentially self-regulating teams.

They have found that team members of these self-regulating teams must be multiskilled. Each team member can do a variety of tasks and rotate jobs with one another at regular intervals, a system that helps reduce boredom and increases motivation.

Employees in these teams are encouraged to learn as much as possible. Gilbert says it takes about three years for a technician on one of these teams to learn all the jobs required to run an operation (Wagel, 1987). To encourage them to learn new skills, they pay them for new skills they acquire. A technician starting out at $21,000 can earn $33,000 after years if he or she progresses on schedule. Once a technician has acquired all the skills, he or she then receives pay raises to stay competitive with other similar jobs in the area. Gilbert noted that they do not have a merit component since trying to differentiate between job performance of two people on a team was not conducive to teamwork (Wagel, 1987).

A key part of their pay-for-knowledge incentive plan is their evaluation system. Initially, technicians on a team each completed written evaluations on each other every six months and gave them to the manufacturing manager, who reviewed them and discussed the results with technicians one-on-one. Eventually, this approach changed so that technicians began reporting evaluations of each other face-to-face. Technicians rate only team members and members of teams who replace them on their shift.

The Bayport facility has found that this system has been effective for it but that such a participative culture is not for everyone. There was a 50 percent turnover during its first two years. Since then, it selection process has improved, and its turnover rate is around 5 percent. Gilbert said it became better at selecting people. It looks for people who exhibit responsibility, versatility, learning ability, honesty, initiative, cooperation, openness, and so on.

Management used the Texas Employment Commission to help test applicants for their ability to learn. High scorers were separately interviewed by two members of management and the technical team where they would be employed. Interviewers then met and agreed on an overall rating. Those who scored the highest were brought back and interviewed by the team, and then the team made the decision to hire or not to hire. Management notes that it used the Texas Employment Commission help to tell members whether they needed to hire someone for EEO (equal opportunity) reasons.

Sometimes a team member does not work out because of too many absences, unexplained tardiness, poor job performance, and so on. In the case of dismissals, team members are involved in the decision.

Today, their teams continue to work on teamwork. They conduct team-building sessions and continue to meet to find ways to improve their communication and cooperation. Effort is still spent dealing with interpersonal skills and ways of enhancing attitudes. The bottom line for Rohm and Haas is that team management has been a key reason for steadily improving quality and lower operating costs.

CONCLUDING THOUGHTS

We have looked at many concepts of team management. It is a simple, but effective, idea for enhancing productivity and employee relations. While the idea of teams may be simple, implementation is not. U.S.

managers from top to bottom have been ingrained with the idea of hierarchy and authoritarian control.

Building teamwork, so essential to effective teams, requires shifting some authority and responsibilities to team members. This change may alienate some traditional managers who felt they will lose authority and responsibility. Despite all the changes, Hoechst Celanese and G.E., among others, show that team management can be used successfully and holds enormous potential for engaging the work force. In the next chapter, we look at how to set up teams so they have the greatest chance at success.

REFERENCES

Alinsworth, Susan. "160 Heads Are Better Than 7." *Reporter* 3, no. 3 (Fall 1989): 16–17.

Alster, Norm. "What Flexible Workers Can Do." *Fortune*, February 13, 1990, 66.

Braun, Kay Bender. "A Tale of Two Teams." *Reporter* 5, no. 1 (Spring 1990): 18–19.

Drucker, Peter F. "Workers' Hands Bound by Tradition." *Wall Street Journal*, August 2, 1988, 2.

Dumaine, Brian. "How Managers Can Succeed Through Speed." *Fortune*, February 13, 1989, 57.

Dwyer, Carol A. "Teamwork Pays Off." *Monogram* 68, no. 2 (Spring 1990): 12–17.

O'Connell, Frances. "Who's on Second? Everyone!" *Reporter* 4, no. 1 (Winter 1990): 8–9.

Stine, Andrea. "Design for Decision Making." *Reporter* 3, no. 2 (July 1989): 7–10.

Wagel, William H. "Working (and Managing) Without Supervisors." *Personnel*, September, 1987, 8–11.

13

Building A Team

Teamwork is an essential part of effective teams. Enrique Sosa, the group vice president for the Chemical and Performance Division of Dow Chemical knows the importance of teamwork. He makes the point that you do not need a team to have teamwork, but you do need teamwork to have a team ("Teamwork" 1990). What exactly does teamwork consist of?

According to Sosa, teamwork consists of several attributes, including the need to make sure the necessary experts are on the teams. The reason is simple: those most familiar with the problem situation should be on the team. Among those attributes that Sosa mentions for good teamwork were the ability of members to compromise and respect for each other's views.

The vice president also says that from a teamwork standpoint, it is necessary not to let individual goals get in the way of team goals. While individual goals are important, they must be compatible with the team goals. In turn, team goals must be compatible with the business and organizational goals. Finally, from a teamwork standpoint, there is no substitute for unity of purpose. Every team must have common purposes and goals.

These same sentiments about the need for a clear purpose and team goals are reiterated by two organizations that have had extensive experience with team management. One of those teams, Ford Motor Company, states that to be effective, a team must have common goals (Ford 1984). Without these shared goals, time and energy are wasted and little will be accomplished.

To build a team purpose, Ford management emphasizes you should ask yourself if your group's goals are clear to all team members. Is everyone trying to achieve the same goal? To help ensure that goals are understood and accepted, each member should have a say in deciding upon those goals, much as the maintenance team did in the last chapter.

DEFINING TEAMS

Metropolitan Life Insurance Company (Met Life) is the other company that has had extensive experience with team management. It has a good definition of a team: a group of people with specific roles and responsibilities, organized to work together toward common goals or objectives, in which each member depends on others to carry out their responsibilities in order to reach team goals and objectives (Metropolitan 1986). That is a pretty good definition of both a team and what a team is trying to accomplish.

Met Life says the key word in its definition is the word *depends*. A team must be able to depend on its members to carry out their tasks. Teams also depend on their members to communicate and listen effectively. Team members must also put the team's needs above their own needs and must help each other. Good teams depend on good team leadership, feedback on their decisions, and common goals and objectives. In other words, as Ford concisely puts it, it is not a team unless it behaves like one (Ford 1984). There must be trust, cooperation, and mutual respect among members. Just how do you build such a team? How do you get one to bond into an effective unit?

It takes team members' knowing their goals and their roles and working out relationships with other team members, but how do you do that? There is no one best way. Sometimes it takes something special for a team to bond. Ford management tells the story of a chief engineer and his group who kept trying, with little success, to clarify their goals, roles, and relationships. At first they tried to do this through regular meetings in his office, but there were constant interruptions. The team then decided it would be best to go off-site for a one-day team development session. Despite some suspicions by some members, they still went. After the meeting, all unanimously agreed it was time well spent. There were better trust, better understanding of goals and roles, and more frequent and open communication (Ford 1984). It was then and only then that they became a team.

TEAM-BUILDING ELEMENTS

Regardless of how a team forms its identity, several elements must be worked out before teams can function with any degree of teamwork. Met Life says that problem solving/team building has three elements:

Figure 13.1
Team-Building Process

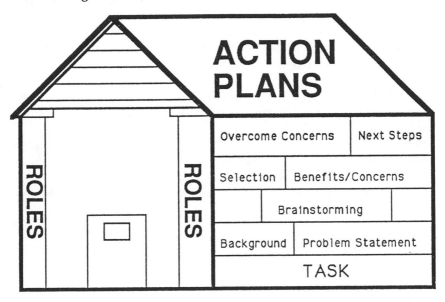

Source: Courtesy of Metropolitan Life Insurance Company

establishing the team's roles, using certain communication techniques, and following a specific problem-solving sequence of steps.

To summarize these points, Met Life shows (as seen in Figure 13.1) that this team-building process can be compared with building a house. Its foundation is the task that brings the group together. The post of this house that supports its walls and roof are the roles team members assume. The bricks that make up the walls are the sequence of steps that teams follow to solve problems. The mortar that holds these bricks together is communication techniques used by the group. Finally, the roof of this symbolic team-building process is the action plan used to implement team ideas and solutions (Metropolitan 1986).

Now we can look at this team building in greater detail.

Roles and Responsibilities

According to Met Life, every team needs to have certain roles assumed by or assigned to its members. Each member of the team should know exactly what role he or she is to play. Only when these roles are clear do teams achieve their goals. In assigning roles, make sure that each team member accepts and is able to handle the responsibility of that role. It is also important to make sure the work load is equitable and no one member is overburdened. Assignments should not just be dumped on people. When too much is required, people feel threatened and may even reject participation or assignments. For this reason, team members should have the opportunity to participate in the assignment of work.

Ford emphasizes that regardless of the purpose of team meetings (setting goals, establishing plans, or solving problems), the best ones are well planned. Ample time should be taken in advance of the meeting to ensure all necessary arrangements have been made. Poor planning produces poor performance.

With good planning, participants have a clear idea of the purpose of the meetings. There will also be better agreement on the agenda and procedures to follow. There are more understanding and commitment to the project. Lastly, and for some most importantly, good planning assures that meetings start on time and end on time.

TEAM LEADERSHIP

The success of team meetings also depends on the team leader's leadership skills. Leaders should be able to supply essential information and clarify issues. Leaders should encourage all members to participate and, at the same time, protect individual members from being attacked. If conflicts do occur, they are resolved quickly. Leaders also help the group stay on track so all issues are heard. Other general criteria for effective team leadership are seen in Figure 13.2.

Met Life provides some concrete suggestions for improving team leadership when it notes that a common approach, but a common weakness of team leadership that leads to failure of the chairperson's leadership, is that one person has responsibilities for two different things: (1) the problem the meeting is supposed to address ("what") and (2) the way the meeting goes ("how") (Metropolitan 1986).

Met Life says giving one person the responsibility for focusing on both what the team is to address and how it goes about that process is a heavy burden. For instance, a leader with both responsibilities may focus so much on resolving a problem that the meeting itself is out of control. As a result, many good ideas can be lost in the shuffle. Met Life's management says its experience shows that when a team leader tries to manage both items, there is a tendency for him or her to lose control or to impose his or her own will and/or there is no participation by others (Metropolitan 1986).

Because of these problems it recommends that team leadership be divided into two roles—client and facilitators (Metropolitan 1986). The client is the team member who asks for assistance in solving a problem; this person is responsible for the "what" of team meetings. Specifically,

Figure 13.2
Characteristics of Effective Team Leaders

Effective leadership is essential to teamwork. Effective leaders can add enormous strength to the process and can have a positive impact on the teamwork climate. Effective team leaders seem to have the following characteristics. They:

- *Understand and willingly accept their obligation to the teamwork process.*
- *Deal fairly and consistently with everyone.*
- *Believe that people want to do a good job.*
- *Are open and forthright and consistently do what they say they will do. When they can't, they explain why not.*
- *Care about people and respect them as individuals.*
- *Believe that when people in their work group do well, they themselves do well; they take pride in the accomplishments of the group they are generous in sharing credit for work the group has performed.*
- *Demonstrate actions consistent with what they expect of others.*
- *Actively solicit ideas and listen carefully when ideas are offered.*
- *Are dedicated to improving people's working lives, to their safety, and to the efficient production of quality products and services.*
- *Actively seek out education, training, and development opportunities for members of the team, including themselves.*
- *Are willing to coach and advise and not rely solely on the authority of their positions.*
- *Keep themselves and members of their teams aware of the needs of other teams and those of internal and external customers.*
- *Meet regularly with their counterparts to openly exchange information and ideas.*
- *Support team efforts, and get help for the team when help is needed.*
- *Strive for continuous improvement--in themselves and in their relationships with people.*
- *Seek out information that pertains to their work groups and regularly pass the information along.*
- *Demonstrate their support for the group and its individual members when things are not going smoothly.*
- *Conduct themselves as professional representatives of their respective organizations, and they do so with pride.*

Source: From *Team, We Are a Team,* an information package. Ford Motor Company, 1988, p. 17 (Used with permission).

the client's role involves (1) providing background information for the team; (2) clearly describing the problem, including identifying what is to be achieved; (3) selecting the most promising ideas provided by the group, so those ideas can be evaluated in greater detail; and (4) completing an action plan. In a moment, we will look at this action plan in greater detail.

Another key team leadership role is what is referred to as the facilitators. This role is responsible for "how" the meeting goes. These facilitators have four basic responsibilities: (1) assisting other team members in keeping time commitments, (2) keeping group members on track, (3) remaining neutral about the content of the meeting, and (4) clarifying ideas of group members to make sure that other members' ideas are protected from attack and premature death (Metropolitan 1986).

Both client and facilitator roles are essential leadership roles, but there are two other essential team roles. One recorder, who does not have leadership responsibilities but does have an essential role, including using flip charts to take notes, so that every member of the group can see what has been agreed on before the meeting is over.

Recorders also are responsible for what Met Life calls "headlining." This involves first noting and then recording key ideas and relevant phrases on a flip chart, using those words agreed upon by the team. Flip charts are used not only to show everyone the key facts and ideas generated but also to help members understand what future steps will be needed. These charts aid problem solving, because they ensure that each person in the group has a uniform record of team efforts. When meetings are finished, these flip charts are typed up and distributed to members.

The remaining role for team members is that of resources. All remaining team members play this role and contribute ideas and provide support for the process. A summary of these roles is seen in Figure 13.3. Met Life notes these roles are the "posts" that support its team structure. To strengthen this structure, Met Life refers to the need to use effective communication techniques, which it calls its "mortar."

COMMUNICATION TECHNIQUES

Interpersonal communication is the key to all members' being able to work together as a team. One reason communication is so important is human nature. Almost anyone who hears of a new idea or approach has a tendency to be skeptical, to look for reasons an idea will not work, or to find something wrong with it. Such negative reactions are natural. Likewise, Met Life points out that people have a tendency to assume there is only one right answer and to try to kill those ideas that do not agree with their own past experience or beliefs. For all these reasons, it

Figure 13.3
Problem Solving/Team Building: Summary of Roles

ROLES	RESPONSIBILITIES
CLIENT:_____	"Owner of the Task: • Provides background information • Formulates problem statement • Selects and prioritizes ideas for group • Accepts ultimate responsibility for completion of the Action Plan
FACILITATOR:_____	"Caretaker of the Process" • Keeps group on process (roles and responsibilities) • Remains in a neutral role vis-vis content • Assists group in keeping to time commitments • Clarifies/paraphrases the contributions made by group members
RECORDER:_____	"Keeper of the 'Group Memory'" • Remains neutral like the facilitator • Writes down key ideas, pertinent phrases and benefits/concerns agreed to by group • Transcribes flip charts to typed format and distributes to the group
RESOURCE:_____	"Contributor of Ideas" • Uses interpersonal skills to assure positive outcome • Generates ideas fully; builds on ideas • Refrains from judging value of client's problems • Works hard to overcome concerns

Source: Courtesy of Metropolitan Life Insurance Company

is important for ideas to be seen as neither totally acceptable nor totally unacceptable.

Met Life uses five interpersonal communication techniques to help its teams improve both communication and problem solving. A summary of these techniques is seen in Figure 13.4. They include reflecting, paraphrasing, using open-ended questions, reacting with benefits before concerns, and headlining. Reflecting involves using statements like, "You're really pleased about that ..." The value of using techniques like reflecting is that it helps the speaker know you understand the emotion or experience being expressed.

Paraphrasing involves restating what has been said with a statement similar to "It sounds to me like you ..." The purpose of such a statement

Figure 13.4
Problem Solving/Team Building: Summary of Communication Techniques

TECHNIQUE	WHAT IT IS
REFLECTING:_____	Crystallizing what a person is saying to let him or her know you are connecting; it is generally used to mirror back to the speaker the emotion or feeling that you--as listener--are experiencing.
	For example, "You're really pleased about that."
PARAPHRASING:_____	Restating what someone has just said to make sure that you have understood what was said.
	For example, "What I hear you saying..."; "it sounds like..."; "it seems like..."
OPEN-ENDED QUESTIONS:_____	Using questions phrased in such a way that they require more than a "yes" or "no" answer. They allow a person to open up and tell you more. They allow you to get more information, to clarify and to obtain feedback.
	These types of questions are formulated by using words like: WHAT, WHERE, HOW and WHY.
REACTING WITH BENEFITS BEFORE CONCERNS:_____	Looking at the strong points of an idea first, before looking at an idea's flaws. In other words, we look at the benefits of an idea before we express our concerns about it.
	This helps to nurture ideas and move past the acceptability threshold, where they become useful, viable ideas.
HEADLINING:_____	Capsulizing an idea in a few succinct words before expanding on it.
	This signals to a listener where the speaker is headed and the point he or she wishes to make, so that the listener's attention is more focused.

Source: Courtesy of Metropolitan Life Insurance Company

is to make sure you do understand what is being said and to make sure the speaker knows you understand.

Using open-ended questions, described in Figure 11.4 involves asking questions that cannot be responded to with a yes or not answer. The reason for using these types of questions is to get people to open up and provide more information and help clarify an issue. Normally, open-ended questions begin with words like what, where, how, and why.

Reacting with benefits before concerns has significant impact on communication. Using this technique encourages group members to look for the strong points of an idea before looking at its drawbacks. In other words, when an idea is presented, the group tries to look at the idea's benefits before focusing on its concerns or drawbacks. The objective of the technique is to try to nurture ideas rather than trying to destroy the problem-solving atmosphere.

Headlining involves trying to summarize an idea with as few key words before expanding on it. The procedure helps people on the team to keep going in the same direction and to know where the discussion is headed.

SEQUENCE OF PROBLEM-SOLVING STEPS

While important, communication alone will not ensure successful team problem solving. Met Life recommends a seven-step sequence be followed to ensure problems are thoroughly resolved. These steps include defining the current situation, formulating the problem statement, brainstorming, selecting ideas, analyzing benefits and concerns, overcoming concerns, and creating an action plan (Metropolitan 1986).

The first step, defining the current situation with background, requires that before decisions are made, the relevant facts and activities that help identify a problem should be stated. This statement should also include a definition of any results that are desired. Met Life says it is the client's role to define the current situation.

Formulating the problem statement involves developing a concise statement beginning with the word *how*. Also included in this problem statement is an action verb that lets everyone in the group know what is to be done, what is expected, and when it is expected.

Brainstorming involves opening up problem solving by considering the thoughts, wishes, and suggestions of team members. Both client and resource people are involved in this step.

Selecting ideas involves taking those ideas generated through brainstorming and further developing them. Facilitators may ask the person acting in the client's role to list these ideas in priority. It is usually the client's role to select the ideas, because the client "owns" the problem.

Met Life says that team members may question why the client has responsibility for selecting the brainstormed idea that should be further evaluated. Some people may also express concern that the client may push a pet idea that is not better than one suggested by other resources. In response, Met Life points out that the next step in the problem-solving process—analyzing the benefits and concerns—helps prevent poor ideas (no matter where they come from) from receiving further evaluation (Metropolitan 1986).

Analyzing the benefits/concerns of ideas involves developing a list of at least three benefits first, then looking at concerns about the ideas. These concerns should be listed in the form of "how to" statements.

Again, benefits are listed before concerns to prevent good ideas from being prematurely killed.

The objective of overcoming concerns is to minimize these concerns by simply stating them as potential problems. As noted above, such concerns need to be framed similarly to "How to . . ." or "I wish . . ." statements. The reason for this procedure, according to Met Life, is to recycle concerns through the sequence of problem-solving steps, so hopefully these problems can be overcome.

The last step in this process is creating an action plan. At this stage, it is assumed that the chosen ideas become the solution to the problem. The action plan contains the specifics about how to resolve the issue, including determining who will do what and by when, how the team will know it accomplished its goals, and when the team needs to get back together (if necessary) (Metropolitan 1986).

A summary of this sequence of problem-solving steps is seen in Figure 13.5. Met Life is happy with this problem-solving sequence but points out that the sequence is not learned by merely discussing it. To enhance problem solving, one must apply the sequence.

Met Life emphasizes that it is extremely important for a team member, in the role of client, to coach team members in the problem solving as it progresses. These individuals should monitor the communication skills used by team members and encourage them to stay on track by following the problem-solving sequence of steps.

Facilitators also have a role of encouraging team members to use this problem-solving sequence by praising them when they apply the steps correctly with statements like, "Thanks for building on that idea." Facilitators can also encourage use of the sequence by simply pointing out when team members should be using it with statements like, "Could you express your concern as a how-to statement?" or "Could you—or someone else—help me to headline that idea?"

When setting up an action plan, make sure to set up a time and place for necessary follow-up meetings to discuss progress and then choose another high-priority problem.

CONCLUDING THOUGHTS

For teams to function effectively, there must be teamwork. Teamwork is not something you just wish for; it must be built into the team process. There must be team goals. The team must have a clear purpose if members are to get a sense of teamwork.

Teams are more than goals and objectives. As Met Life says, good teams consist of people with specific roles and responsibilities who depend on each other to achieve those goals. It takes good planning and

Figure 13.5
Problem Solving/Team Building: Summary of Sequence of Steps

ACTIVITY		BRIEF DESCRIPTION
STEP 1:	DEFINING CURRENT SITUATION WITH BACKGROUND	State relevant facts and activities which help identify that a problem exists. Include prior actions or thoughts that have already been considered and define the results desired by using this problem solving process.
STEP 2:	FORMULATING THE PROBLEM STATEMENT	Develop a concise action statement begininning with "How to;" include an action verb that denotes accomplishment and state what we expect done and when we expect it. (How much? How soon?)
STEP 3:	BRAINSTORMING	Open up the problem solving by developing thoughts, wishes, suggestions and action recommendations on how to accomplish the objective identified.
STEP 4:	SELECTING IDEAS	Select a single idea or group of ideas for further development. Sometimes, if all ideas are promising, the facilitator asks the client to prioritize them.
STEP 5:	ANALYZING THE BENEFITS/CONCERNS	Develop a list of at least three benefits, before listing your concerns. Phrase concerns as potential problems in "How to" statements. For example, "How to get the resources we need to implement this idea."
STEP 6:	OVERCOMING CONCERNS	Generate ideas to overcome any concerns which must be addressed before the selected idea can be implemented. In other words, recycle concerns through the sequence of steps as new problems, if necessary.
STEP 7:	CREATING THE ACTION PLAN	Identify the "next steps," which will assure that the chosen idea becomes a solution to the problem. During the process the individual (or group) identifies next activities, and sets up appropriate controls to monitor progress and communicate results.

Source: Courtesy of Metropolitan Life Insurance Company

good team leadership to ensure that all members are happy with the group and their own role.

Met Life believes one of the reasons teams are ineffective and lack teamwork is that a few people try to do too many things. It suggests that to ensure effectiveness, the team should be divided into client, facilitator, recorder, and resources roles. It is then essential that a wide range of interpersonal communication techniques be used to ensure ideas are thoroughly explored. Finally, building a good team depends on following a specific sequence of problem-solving steps.

REFERENCES

Ford Education and Personnel Research Development. *Continuous Improvement Through Participation*. September 1984, 6.

Metropolitan Life Insurance Company. *The National Work Team Leaders Guide to the Quality Improvement Process*. 1986, 37.

"Teamwork—More Critical Today Than Ever Before." *Quality Performance* 7, no. 9 (May 31, 1990): 2.

14

Open Communication

A great deal of management's current concern for employee productivity and the need to empower people has revolved around the use of teams. No doubt teams have enhanced both productivity and employee relations, but one should never assume teams are the only or even right way to empower people. Sometimes individual effort, rather than group effort, is needed. Sometimes what is needed is the simplest of all needs—communication.

In a 1990 study, industrial engineers were asked how to improve productivity. Communication concerns drew the strongest response of any question on the survey. Over 88 percent of those surveyed strongly agreed that the lack of communication and cooperation among different components of a business leads to reduced productivity ("P and Q" 1990).

Executive CEOs have also recognized the importance of communication. A study by A. Foster Higgins and Company, an employee-benefits consulting firm, found that 97 percent of the CEOs surveyed believe communicating with employees has a positive impact on job satisfaction. Furthermore, the survey found that 79 percent think it benefits the bottom line, but surprisingly only 22 percent actually do it weekly or more (Farnham 1989). Executives think communicating is extremely important to the success of their business, but they do not do it. It is difficult to understand why this situation exists.

Perhaps the reason is that many CEOs and other top officials prefer the company of their peers to the company of those who do not share the same perspective. Perhaps, like generals on the battlefield, they are more fascinated with strategy than with how those directives are carried out. Regardless of the reason, it is extremely rare to find CEOs or other top officials who actively seek a down-in-the-trenches perspective.

An exception to the normal situation is the approach used by Alabama Gas's CEO, Mike Warren. When Warren became CEO, he found the relations with the company's union in poor repair (Farnham 1989). In a bit of showmanship, he used a 20-foot papier-mâché dinosaur with a stake plunged through its heart. He then wheeled the corpse around from department to department. The message was that the old ways of conducting business were over.

Of course, if all he had done was to go around the departments with a papier-mâché dinosaur, everyone would have thought of the stunt as only hype. Follow-through was critical. He started eating dinner regularly with union leaders. If he was out driving and saw workers laboring in a ditch, he got out and visited with them. He surveyed employees and solicited their suggestions (Farnham 1989). Such actions may appear hokey, but Warren and others say they have had a dynamic effect on their employee relations and productivity. The key to such an approach appears to be whether employees see it as manipulation or as an honest desire to communicate and understand their viewpoint.

TRANSFER OF MANAGEMENT PRACTICES

Communication is both the solution and the problem. Communication within companies continues to be an age-old problem, but some radical, new solutions may help. Most organizations consist of departments resembling a crude caste system, with each area insulating itself from other functional areas. These perceptual walls separate design engineering from production and production from marketing and so forth.

Communication solutions today revolve around much greater data sharing and exchange of information among departments and within them. As already noted, there are wide uses of teams today. Something called concurrent engineering is one such team approach that involves bringing in a wider range of departments and people into the product and production design stage. There are also several ways that open communication can be used to enhance employee relations and productivity.

One such example of a company's using open communication as a competitive weapon is General Electric. G.E. is a diversified organization consisting of 14 divisions, with business involved in aircraft engineering, medical systems, engineering, plastics, major appliances, and even NBC television station and financial services. If there was ever a risk of communication problems, it would be in this $55 billion organization.

Recognizing the need constantly to keep improving, G.E.'s management has experimented with team management and with programs for

eliminating and simplifying work procedures through a program referred to in an earlier chapter as Work Out. One particularly effective
system it uses is called "integrated diversity" (Quickel 1990). It is a term
Jack Welch, G.E.'s CEO, uses to describe how G.E. tries to coordinated
its 14 separate businesses.

The idea behind integrated diversity is that each business division is
supposed to help each other, as opposed to operating separate fiefdoms.
Welch notes that most diversified companies do a good job of transferring technical resources and dollars across their business and some do
a good job of transferring human resources. He says he feels G.E. does
the best job of transferring management practices across its business,
including transferring the best techniques, the best systems, and the
best generic management principles that produce growth and profitability (Quickel 1990).

G.E. is able to transfer these management practices and enhance cooperation and communication through several means. One of the sim-
plest means it uses to improve communication is the linkage with the
CEO. G.E. has its 14 separate business leaders report directly to the
CEO or his two vice-chairmen. This procedure helps eliminate com-
munication problems since it allows direct communication between the
CEO and the leaders of the 14 businesses. As a result, there are very
short cycle times for decisions and little interference by corporate staff.
Welch says decisions that sometimes took a year now take a few days
(Tichy and Charan 1989).

CORPORATE EXECUTIVE COUNCIL

G.E. also runs what it calls its Corporate Executive Council (CEC).
The CEC meets for two days each quarter with 30 or 40 senior executives
from G.E.'s 14 businesses. Rather than a formal review, CEC's meetings
are more informal in nature. The emphasis is on sharing information
and ideas in an open manner. At the end of these two days, everyone
in the CEC meetings has seen and discussed the same information about
both successes and failures.

G.E. feels the CEC creates a sense of trust, personal familiarity, and
mutual obligation at the top of the company. Welch notes that executives
at the CEC meeting do not approve the details of their businesses' plans
and programs, like their pay plans, drug testing, or stock option plans.
Rather, they just want to know the details so all G.E. management can
see which plans are working (Tichy and Charan 1989).

G.E. obviously feels its CEC meetings are an important tool for developing better understanding and coordination among its top officials.
Presentations and meetings of the CEC are only one way G.E. transfers
the best management practices. At lower levels, the same transfer of

information is taking place. Every January, G.E. top managers gather for two and one-half days in Boca Raton, Florida, for cross-pollination. In addition to formal presentations, there are discussions in hotel rooms, cocktail lounges, and locker rooms (Quickel 1990). Informally, managers and their counterparts and peers in other businesses share stories, successes, and problems.

Later in October of each year, a more select group of the top 100 G.E. bosses attend another two and one-half–day session in Phoenix. These sessions are more strategic in nature. Questions at these meetings revolve around competition, acquisition opportunities, and so forth.

While conducting managerial meetings is obviously important, it is not so much the meetings themselves, but rather the way they are conducted that is most significant. For instance, in a 1986 meeting of G.E.'s top 100 executives, 14 business leaders were asked to present reports on various competitive aspects of their business. G.E. had executives present one-page answers to five questions. Concerning global market dynamics and what their competitors were doing and would be doing in the next three years to counteract those threats. They also kept charts and updated the charts related to those questions. Again the purpose was communication, so that everyone at the top knew at a glance what needed to be done (Tichy and Charan 1989).

COMMUNICATION THROUGH GOALS

G.E.'s experience with greater open communication at the top has helped it integrate its diverse culture better. It is the key to being better able to transfer management's best practices from one business to another.

While open communication enhances corporate-level effectiveness, it appears its greatest impact can be at the operational level. Consider the case of Cypress Semiconductor Corporation, located in San Jose, California. It uses a system of goal setting and evaluation that helps focus the corporation through "collective thinking." CEO and founder T. J. Rodgers says that Cypress collects and shares information in such detail that, for all practical purposes, the company can be considered virtually "transparent" (Rodgers 1990). He said that such an open process helps prevent political infighting.

Cypress uses several such systems that it feels makes it more competitive. It feels that its systems help it hire better employees as well as keep them by rewarding outstanding efforts. It also feels its system of goal setting helps allocate resources better.

Cypress's system consists of a series of goal-setting meetings, developing reports, and getting approval for goals that were set. It uses a software package to help managers through a step-by-step process; the package even recommends salary figures, which can be modified within limits.

In addition to using computer software, Cypress puts a lot of emphasis on meeting quarterly revenue and profit targets. To ensure that it meets its goals, it tracks product shipments and revenues on a daily basis (Rodgers 1990). It constantly evaluates how it is measuring up to its quarterly revenue plans and makes changes when needed.

Rodgers says he is less concerned with meeting product-by-product forecasts than with reacting immediately to competitive changes. He says CEOs need detailed information on such things as revenues per employee and how they compare with the records of their competition. He also says they need information on how many orders are delinquent, what their yields are, and, among other things, cycle time at every manufacturing operation (Rodgers 1990). The purpose is not interference, but rather understanding. If a CEO does not understand the basic operational detail of a business, that business is in trouble.

Cypress ensures open communication by collecting detailed operational information, reviewing it regularly, and sharing it widely. This process helps it to set realistic goals. While Cypress's 1,400 employees all have goals, what makes its system different is that every week they set their goals, enter them into their corporate database, and then report whether they were achieved or not.

Project Goals

Cypress organizes most of its work around projects rather than by strict functional lines. The goal-setting process is organized around those projects rather than by function. At Monday's project meeting, short-term goals are set and ranked according to priority. Normally, the goals that are set take from one to six weeks to complete. That same night all project goals are fed into a computer. Tuesday, functional managers receive a printout that shows new and pending goals. They use these computer printouts for their own meetings on Tuesday afternoon. The purpose is to anticipate any problems that might occur, so they know how to overcome them.

On Wednesday, eight vice-presidents review goal printouts for their people. These vice-presidents watch for "delinquency" rates (the percentage of those goals not being met). Rodgers says delinquency rates above 20 percent for managers and 30 percent for vice presidents would be of concern.

The goal of the process is to find out how to help improve the operation. To that end, Cypress provides feedback to individuals. Each month it issues a Completed Goal Report for every person in the company. This report shows all goals completed and those yet to be completed over the last four weeks. Cypress uses the report for a performance minireview every month. By the year's end, it has a dozen such objective reports to use for its final evaluation.

COMPUTER-INTEGRATED BUSINESS

A great deal of Cypress's goal-setting process and open communication is dependent on computer technology. Although computer technology does not necessarily lead to open communication, it certainly has the potential to do so. Increasingly, companies are referring to something called "computer-integrated business." Its potential to impact productivity and communication is enormous.

In theory, computer-integrated business involves sales, finance, distribution, and manufacturing openly exchanging information quickly and constantly via the computer (Main 1990). Product designers can send specifications directly to machines on the factory floor. Salespeople and customers can find what they want in stock, when it can be delivered, and when they can place orders. Likewise, accounting and others can receive on-line information about sales, purchases, and prices. Executives are immediately updated and have access to a wide variety of operational information.

In theory, this procedure sounds good. In practice, it is difficult to implement fully. Computer networks are at various stages of development throughout a company. There are some shining examples of some aspects of computer networks.

Frito-Lay, PepsiCo's most profitable division, provides hand-held Fujitsu computers to every one of its 10,000 route salespeople, who carry them into stores. Salespeople then punch the code number and quantity of Frito products that need to be replaced. At the end of the day, all 10,000 salespeople book their hand-helds to telephones, and the information is sent to their mainframes in Dallas. Data are then redistributed to those areas that need the information. President Robert Beeby, as well as area and division heads, can know precisely how their sales are doing.

This process eliminates paperwork and provides better information about what is occurring in the field. It shows what is working and what is not working on a store-by-store basis. Supporters of this computer system say that it provides CEOs and others with better knowledge of what is going on. In turn, CEOs will tend to feel more comfortable allowing lower-level managers a freer hand. Those lower-level managers will also have the knowledge to make better decisions.

COMMUNICATION THROUGH KNOWLEDGE

With all the talk about computers, it is important to remember that they are not the only means available for opening up communication. Open communication also figures into Wal-Mart's success. Upper management makes a point of exchanging ideas with store personnel. Ralph Graham, a store manager, said the company is continuously asking for ideas on how to improve its operation. It expects high performance and openly shows its department managers, as well a store managers, what each of their areas is doing. Graham also noted: "We share our store sales, profits, losses, purchase mark-up, rate of inventory, turnover and so on. There isn't a figure we keep from our department managers." Each month departments also list what they grossed and how they compared with the rest of the stores in the same region. If they rank better than the average, they are given a bonus; if not, the department tries to correct its performance.

Jack Stack believes much of his company's (Springfield Remanufacturing Corporation [SRC]) success and of the commitment of its employees is due in large part to its communication and human relations effort. SRC believes employees will be committed when they have a basic understanding of how and why the company operates as it does. To that end it teaches all employees about finance and accounting, often even before they completely master their job. Stack says, "We teach them about finance and accounting before they turn a wrench" (Denton, 1988, 17). Ile believes if they knew what he and management did, they would make the same decision.

In particular, SRC uses budgets and income statements much as Cypress uses its goal-setting process. Every week the company reviews its income statements with all employees and managers. The discussion includes a detailed analysis of each department's financial condition, including line-by-line financial positive and negative variances.

Using this analysis, top managers set their financial goals. In turn, department managers take these data and go through the same analysis with their employees. Such a detailed analysis provides even the lowest-level employees with a comprehensive picture of what it takes to make money and what each contributes to the profit-and-loss statement. To encourage ownership of the process, this employee-owned and operated business sets department financial goals and offers sizable bonuses for those who beat the standard.

Educating employees about finances is only one way SRC communicates with its employees. This communication process, as at Wal-Mart, is ingrained. SRC managers know all their employees. They know them on a first name and personal basis. They try to talk to them, not at them, by having an open-door policy and encouraging employees to ask questions. Communication at SRC is positive, and as Stack stated, "We have incredible people—every single one of them." Stack's commitment to his employees has helped produce a climate of trust and enthusiasm.

SRC is not the only organization that has been able to secure employee commitment through openly sharing information. Wal-Mart, along with other organizations, puts special emphasis on management and employees openly sharing information about both business and many personal aspects of their lives. Information about profits, growth, problems, "hot items," and the Wal-Mart family is openly shared. The attitude is, "Just thought you would like to know." This openness is seen in many of its individual stores. One store manager said he openly shares information about how each department is doing. He noted that no figure is withheld from department heads, including information on sales, profits, losses, markup, and inventory.

SIMPLE ACCESS

If the approaches of SRC and Cypress are too revolutionary for you, consider getting started by simple access. Openly sharing information is also used by another successful firm, Litton:ACD (Advanced Circuitry Division). It is one of the top three companies among 1,800 competitors and gives a lot of credit for its success to its emphasis on open and informal communication. Don Moore, the personnel director, says there is no price tag for well-informed employees. He believes everyone needs to feel a part of the organization and wants to know what is going on. To this end Litton:ACD conducts monthly communication meetings both to inform and to solve problems, to explain layoffs or videotape topics of interest to employees, to explain a particular customer's philosophy or attitudes, and to tell employees why goods from customers were returned or why a specific complaint was made.

Litton:ACD also uses other means of keeping the communication open between employees and management, including monthly "coffees" when the general manager meets with various groups within the plant to discuss anything that is on their minds. An ombudsman and the open-door policy of the Personnel Department also encourage employees' communication.

Another organization carries this open-door policy a step further by locating the personnel office in the middle of the factory floor instead of in the "ivory tower" near the president. A great deal more informal contact has been established with employees since those barriers have been reduced.

Every three years 3M Corporation randomly mails a questionnaire to one out of every four employees. On one of the two off years, the local plants conduct their own similar survey. Both surveys cover a wide range of topics, including training, promotion, job satisfaction, working conditions, and compensation concerns. While many companies conduct surveys, 3M is more effective than most. It has a 78 percent response rate (most companies feel lucky if they get a low 40s rate.) Why the high return rate? Because most employees feel their opinions do matter. The human resource manager said, "Employees feel satisfaction from answering the questions."

Why do they feel satisfaction? Because the company appears to listen to them. In the past, the survey has been used to make a wide range of changes from benefit programs to working conditions. The opinion surveys not only provide 3M with an opportunity to show employees that it is listening but also give it an opportunity to emphasize the family attitude that 3M encourages.

Other 3M communication vehicles include its Between-Us program, which allows individuals anonymously to express concerns they have. Another program, called Skip-ONE, encourages open communication by allowing employees occasionally to skip their boss. It is informal and not performance-related but allows individuals to get acquainted with their supervisor's boss. A boss also gets to know his or her subordinate's employees. Speak Up Meetings also encourage open communication. At various times of the year employees are encouraged to come to a meeting with the plant manager, who lets employees know of the company's progress, problems, and challenges.

CONCLUDING THOUGHTS

There are many ways to open up communication. It is essential that companies consider some of those mentioned here or develop their own. It is essential because of the powerful impact that open communication has on productivity and employee relations. Of course, that impact should not be unexpected. Anything that improves employee relations tends to improve productivity.

Open communication comes in many forms. The form is not as important as the philosophy of openly sharing and trusting others with critical information. Everyone communicates, some more openly than others. The greater the sharing, the greater the rewards for both employees and corporation as a whole. Next, we will look specifically at how to communicate in an open manner in face-to-face situations.

REFERENCES

Denton, D. Keith. "Better Management Through Budgeting: Instilling a Quality Culture," *Management Review*, October 1988, 16–18.

Farnham, Alan. "The Trust Gap." *Fortune*, December 4, 1989, 70.
Main, Jeremy. "Computers of the World Unite!" *Fortune*, September 24, 1990, 115.
"P and Q Survey." *Focus* (*Industrial Engineering*) 1990, 6.
Quickel, Stephen W. "Welch on Welch." *Financial World* 159, no. 7 (April 3, 1990): 3.
Rodgers, T. J. "No Excuses Management." *Harvard Business Review*, July–August 1990, 85.
Tichy, Noel, and Ram Charan. "Speed, Simplicity, Self-Confidence." *Harvard Business Review*, September-October 1989, 115.

15

Merck's Face-To-Face Communication

Fewer than half of the employees polled in a 1990 study by Towers Perrin, a consulting firm, believed management is aware of the problems they face. Research by the Hay Group that covered 1 million employees in over 2,000 organizations found that only 34 percent responded favorably to questions about how well their company listened to them (Rice 1991). Employees want to hear from management, and they want management to listen to them. *Fortune* reports that the best managers spend up to 40 percent of their time in face-to-face encounters with their employees (Rice 1991).

There are as many styles of face-to-face communication as there are styles of leadership. Mike Walsh, the CEO who changed Union Pacific from a sluggish hierarchical company to a successful and progressive one, holds face-to-face meetings for five and one-half hours with employees from 24 sites. Via satellite, employees fire questions at him covering everything from workplace safety to job security. It is an informal affair that seems to suit his style. Before he came, Union Pacific was more formal, with "Mr." and "Mrs." titles before names. Now, first names prevail, and cross-functional teams are common.

A more informal and effective face-to-face communication style was established when Walsh held so-called town meetings with 300 to 1,000 employees per session. In these meetings he explained the company's strategy and recent industry changes, but most importantly, he asked employees for their ideas. Today, he still has such meetings plus frequent sessions with smaller groups of 15 to 20 employees. He says a CEO must be "visible, vulnerable, and willing to put himself on the line. It is also essential to tell the truth and demonstrate that you share employees' concerns, even when you can't do much about them" (Rice 1991, 112).

Welch's style seems sincere. John Amerman, the CEO for Mattel, seems just as sincere, but maybe with a bit more showmanship. Amerman wanted to make work (and communicating) more fun, so he once announced quarterly results by putting the message in a rap routine that he delivered to assembled workers backed up by a group of secretaries called the Rappettes (Rice 1991).

The personable CEO began his job at Mattel by informing employees that work should be more fun. He asked for their help and asked them to try to enjoy work more. He began his face-to-face meetings by wandering around, eating in the cafeteria, and, like Walsh, meeting regularly with employees. He asked for suggestions on how to eliminate layers within the organization and cut six layers from the hierarchy. He speaks to employees without a written script but develops a "structured format" in his mind and rehearses what he is going to say.

It was in 1989 that he announced earnings with a rap routine. The next year, he had his two lieutenants put on a Las Vegas–style revue. All wore tuxedos and glittery top hats and called themselves the "Toy Boys." They danced and sang new lyrics to old tunes (e.g., "There's No Business Like Toy Business"). They brought down the house when at the end of the show, they announced that all 1,100 rank-and-file headquarter employees would receive a bonus of two weeks' pay that was to come out of seven managers' bonus pool.

More sedate is Bob Crawford, CEO of Brook Furniture Rental, who wants to create an atmosphere where employees speak openly. He says, "People will put every effort into advancing the business if they can communicate their ideas" (Rice 1991, 112). Crawford believes in the power of interpersonal communication and of the personal touch. He especially believes that listening is the most powerful communication tool. He urges his staff to listen carefully to what both their customers and employees are saying. Listen first before imparting information. This point may have best been described by J. Stark Thompson, CEO of Life Technologies, who said, "I've learned just because you think it, write it, or say it doesn't mean employees hear it or believe it" (Rice 1991, 17).

All of this communicating may be fine if you are a CEO, but if you are not, what can you do? That is what this chapter is about. There are practical techniques you can use to enhance your effectiveness and that of your face-to-face meetings.

NUTS AND BOLTS

Open communication is more than a philosophy. It consists of specific procedures, techniques, and skills. The rest of this chapter discusses the nuts and bolts of communication and provides examples of when and how to use Face-to-Face communication.

One company that has made effective use of Face-to-Face communication, Merck, the giant pharmaceutical company, is widely recognized both for its success and for its outstanding employee relations. It is routinely recognized as one of the best-run and best-managed American companies. One of the tools it uses to enhance employee relations and productivity is Face-to-Face communication. These meetings are a vital part of its communication efforts.

In the following pages we will look at Merck's approach and make specific suggestions, but remember these are merely suggestions and should not be thought of as a set of concrete rules. These suggestions should be modified to suit your own needs. The purpose is to ensure that Face-to-Face communication meetings between you and your employees are as productive as possible.

PURPOSE

All employees need and even want to meet personally with their managers, and Face-to-Face meetings accomplish this goal. A smooth flow of information is difficult, if not impossible, without a formal communication program. Merck's Face-to-Face communication meetings are designed to open up communication within the company and improve the flow of information among the levels of management and between managers and their employees.

A systematic approach toward Face-to-Face meetings ensures that managers and employees are able to discuss mutual concerns. Meetings like these can help both sides understand the needs and goals of the other. They can also be used to discuss business issues openly and to provide employees with more information about the company.

These meetings can be conducted by different levels of managers ranging from top executives to supervisors. At Merck, Face-to-Face meetings last about one to two hours and are informal in nature. One purpose of these meetings is so information can be shared and everyone can understand management's concerns and goals. Remember, it is a two-way communication process in which management should also become aware of the needs and concerns of employees.

The rationale for these meetings is simple. When each side understands the other, realistic decisions can be made and realistic goals can be set. Employees are more likely to do a better job because they know what is expected of them, and managers can do a better job of leading if they better understand their people. Face-to-Face meetings are preventative in nature. The understanding you get from Face-to-Face meetings can help you identify and discuss problem areas before they become roadblocks to effective management.

Merck recommends for its own people that if managers have eight or more employees (exempt as well as nonexempt) working with them, they should have these communication sessions three times a year (*A Manager's*) To be effective, these meetings must have the full support of your manager as well as upper management. At Merck the question of support for these meetings is clear, and it has the best possible evidence that these meetings are supported by upper management: the chairman of the Board, the CEO, the president, and the chief operating officers all conduct their own communication meetings with subordinates.

FOUR RULES

Managers considering running a communication meeting should keep themselves focused on two objectives. The first is providing their employees with information they need to do their job better, including information related to the concerns and issues facing the business. Secondly, it is just as important to remember to use these meetings to understand better the needs, concerns, and feelings of employees. This objective is not going to be accomplished if you spend all your time telling and explaining. Better understanding of their needs can come about only in a participative environment.

Face-to-Face meetings must be participative if they are to accomplish both objectives. Information needs to be provided, but there must be time for answering questions and, most importantly, for listening. Merck recommends that four basic rules be used to guarantee more successful meetings (*A Manager's*).

The first of these rules is always to be candid. Questions and comments should be addressed truthfully. If, for some reason, a question cannot be answered because of its confidential or proprietary nature, then say so. Likewise, if you do not know the answer, then say so. Then, if possible, make a commitment to find out the answer and get back to the person.

Second, Merck recommends that when conducting these meetings, you should be well prepared. One of the best ways to be prepared is to invite participants to submit questions or topics for discussion several weeks before the meeting is to occur. Merck's management believes there are two advantages to this procedure. First, it lets you know what is of interest to your employees. Second, it makes it easier for participants to ask tough questions to which they want answers when they might otherwise not have the courage to ask them in the meeting. If you let participants send in their questions anonymously, you will eliminate a great deal of fear and apprehension. You will more likely get the more difficult questions and concerns out in the open, one of the reasons for Face-to-Face meetings.

The third criterion of effective meetings is to encourage participation. In the best meetings everyone is at ease and is encouraged to participate. Obviously, one way to encourage participation is to be open and frank in your own discussions with employees. Merck has found out that one way of breaking the ice is by taking on the tough questions first, perhaps by responding to presubmitted questions. Encouraging others to challenge answers or to ask for clarification when they need it also encourages participation.

The fourth rule is to focus on listening but not judging. If you want open communication, try never to appear upset, dismayed, or judgmental. Never talk down to participants. Probably the single best way to encourage open communication is simply to treat people as adults. No question should be thought of as irrelevant, so listen carefully. Treat others with respect. This is good advice, but difficult to do.

CONDUCTING MEETINGS

A good meeting is impossible unless you are prepared for it. Merck recommends that about three or four weeks before the meeting you should choose participants and a place and time for the meeting. If possible, Merck tries to avoid setting up Monday or Friday meeting dates. It also says to avoid early morning or late evening, since people tend to pay less attention during these times.

Make sure key people attend. Participants should be sent invitations that include the time, date, location, and purpose of the meeting, as well as an RSVP request. An example of a typical invitation is seen in Figure 15.1.

These invitations should include a form for anonymous, presubmitted questions or topics that are of interest to employees who will attend, these Face-to-Face meetings. An example of one such form is seen in Figure 15.2. These forms should include information about the deadline for submitting topics and the name of the person who will be answering the questions.

The reason for the presubmitted questions is the same as for having Face-to-Face meetings—creating an open and honest dialogue. Such questions also help managers become better aware of concerns of their employees. Even distributing information presents opportunities to improve things.

As you receive these presubmitted questions, you should begin to find out the answers yourself or assign someone to develop background information so the questions can be answered. The only risk of delegating this task is to make sure it is not further delegated to the point

Figure 15.1
Sample Invitation

MEMO

TO	PARTICIPANT'S NAME	DEPARTMENT	MAIL CODE
FROM	MANAGER	DEPARTMENT	MAIL CODE
SUBJECT	FACE-TO-FACE MEETING INVITATION		DATE

I am planning a Face-to-Face meeting with (selected) persons from our organization and I would like you to be among the participants. The meeting will be informal in nature and will begin promptly at _(time)_ on _(date)_ in the _(location)_.

This meeting is designed to provide an opportunity for a candid and open discussion of the business issues and concerns in our area. Naturally, the success of this meeting will depend on free and honest questions and answers. I want to talk about and hear your views on the critical issue that management must address in meeting with our Company (Division, Department, etc.) objectives.

Enclosed with this letter is a form you can use anonymously to suggest topics or questions you want addressed at the meeting. I ask only that the questions or topics be broad, tough, and relevant.

If you want to raise more than one issue, please copy the form and use one per question or subject. It is not necessary to sign the form. Questions will also be solicited from the floor. All major topics will be addressed. Please return the form to me as soon as possible and no later than _(deadline)_.

I am looking forward to your active participation in this meeting. If you are unable to attend, please inform me as soon as possible.

Attachments

Source: Courtesy of Merck & Company

that the request eventually ends upon the desk of the one asking the question. Merck says that a good rule is to delegate answering questions only to those who report directly to you (*A Manager's*). Set definite dates for getting all questions answered. Prepare lists of those items participants want answered and hand them out during the meeting. When answers to those questions are prepared, make sure they are accurate, clear, and brief. Avoid rambling, vague, or evasive responses. Naturally,

Figure 15.2
Sample Question/Topic Form

A QUESTION OR TOPIC I WOULD LIKE TO SEE ADDRESSED AT THE FACE-TO-FACE
MEETING IS _____

_____

_____

_____

_____

_____

_____

_____

_____

_____

_____

_____

_____

YOU MAY SUBMIT THIS ANONYMOUSLY.

Please return this form(s) by _____ (date) _____

to: _____(manager's name)_____ , _____ (location) _____

Source: Courtesy of Merck & Company

if sensitive information is to be discussed, make sure appropriate precautions have been taken.

Membership

Take care to invite participants who will profit most from the meeting. Participants of Face-to-Face meetings should be representative of the entire group. Managerial functions, related disciplines, professionals, employees, females, and minorities should be adequately represented if the meeting is to reflect your work force accurately. To have a proper mix, Merck randomly selects participants from its employee roster. For instance, you might choose every second or third name from that roster.

Conducting a Face-to-Face meeting with a mixed audience creates a real opportunity for open communication. Separating or segregating meetings might cause some to become suspicious. Some might wonder, "Exactly what is going on in the other group?" or "What are they being told?"

Merck has found out that cross-functional, multilevel groups provide several benefits, including encouraging better understanding of each other's needs. It also says this process helps everyone better understand the goals of the organization. The advantages of cross-functional communication meetings are many, but there will be times when you will want to meet with a specific group or portion of a group. If your department is small enough, you might want to hold a meeting with the entire group.

PREPARATION

Once you have decided to conduct a communication meeting, you will need to choose a location. You will want to choose a site at or close to work. Make sure the room is the right size. For instance, auditoriums are no good if you are only going to be meeting with 20 or 30 people. Conference rooms that seat 30 are no good if 50 participants are expected. If audiovisual equipment is used, make sure the room lights can be lowered. Check how many tables and chairs will be needed. Merck also says that about three days before the meeting, you should prepare a booklet containing an agenda, prepared remarks, and a list of submitted questions. These questions should contain background information for responding to them.

Face-to-Face meetings are usually opened with a brief welcome, followed by an explanation about what you hope the meeting accomplishes. Merck then follows with a brief 15- to 30-minute talk on a particular subject. Subjects might be a general overview of the business or involve more specific discussion on, for example, company goals, cost measures, new product introduction, or a wide range of other changes. A sample topic list of one communication meeting is seen in Figure 15.3. Subject matter for the meeting really depends on the needs of both management and employees. For that reason managers frequently review presubmitted questions to help determine relevant subjects.

PROCEDURES

All the preparation in the world will not do you any good unless procedures are in place that maximize the potential of the meeting. One of the first things that needs to be worked out is who is in charge. If you use films, slides, or other visual aids as part of the meeting, make

Figure 15.3
Topics to Be Addressed

BUSINESS GOALS

- Productivity
- Budget issues
- New Products
- New Programs
- Reorganization
- Communication

COMPENSATION AND BENEFITS

- Job evaluation
- Merck's salaries as compared to those of other companies

AFFIRMATIVE ACTION

- Company (Division, Department) progress
- Goals and commitment
- Perception (too fast, too slow)

CAREER GROWTH

- Career development
- Performance reviews
- Career opportunities

> **PLEASE NOTE:** This is an example of a Topic List that might be used by a senior manager. The Topic List for your meeting will depend upon the information needs of you and your group. Or you may wish to omit the Topic List and give the participants copies of all pre-submitted questions.

Source: Courtesy of Merck & Company

sure everyone understands you are the leader. You can do this in simple ways. Telling participants that they will be seeing a film and that a question-and-answer discussion will follow lets everyone know who is in charge and the theme of the meeting. Knowing this information helps participants because they can then begin thinking of questions they want to ask.

After the film or lecture, begin the process of two-way communication by having participants ask questions. When appropriate, emphasize that the meeting is meant as a forum for addressing participants' concerns on tough business issues. Sometimes participation can be slow, so it may be necessary to use an icebreaker. One way is first to answer some of the more difficult or hard-hitting presubmitted questions.

When taking questions from participants, be sure you understand those questions. This may sound like simple advice, but questions can be easy to misunderstand. The easiest way to help ensure you understand what is being asked is to repeat the question. A restatement phrase could be used to ensure understanding also. One such phrase might be, "As I understand it, you would like to know. . . ." or "What you're asking me is. . . ."

One other procedure Merck finds effective involves how questions are answered. It says that unless you are quoting company policy, it is best not to read the answers to presubmitted questions. Reading answers gives the impression that they are not your own but are rather prerecorded and not meant to be challenged or questioned.

No one should be expected to have all the answers all the time. If someone asks a question that you cannot honestly answer or the question involves a subject with which you are unfamiliar, then say something like, "I'm not sure; I'll have to get back to you on that in a few days." While it is best to be specific about exactly when you will get back to the questioner with an answer, it is essential that you do get back with the person. Otherwise, you will damage your legitimacy.

Not having a few answers can even be good for your image. It shows that you are human. If, as sometimes occurs, you are uncertain about an answer, then promise to find out and share it with the questioner or the group if they are interested. Never evade or you will lose credibility. It is corny, but an open and honest approach is always the best long-term solution.

As mentioned earlier, another approach to handling an unfamiliar question is to refer it to a staff member. If questions are referred to staff members, then naturally those same people should be aware that they will be called upon to clarify an issue. If questions cannot be answered because of security reasons, then honestly say so. A typical statement might sound something like, "I'm sorry but that deals with confidential information." The point is that your response should be honest and not a way of evading difficult questions.

In any meeting, there are time limits. There are only so many questions that can be answered. If time does run out before all presubmitted questions are answered, tell participants they will receive written responses within one week; then make sure you follow up.

At the end of the meeting, each participant should be asked to fill out an evaluation form similar to that in Figure 15.4. Later, these forms should be reviewed so you can assess the success of the meeting and help improve future meetings. Results of this evaluation may sometimes be disturbing, but remember the purpose is to open communication and

Figure 15.4
Sample Meeting Evaluation Form

COMMUNICATION MEETING: PARTICIPANT EVALUATION

	(Check one)	MOSTLY	PARTLY	SLIGHTLY
Did you feel the meeting was informative?		_____	_____	_____

COMMENTS: _____

_____

Did you feel the questions were answered candidly?   _____   _____   _____

COMMENTS: _____

_____

Did you feel free to ask questions?   _____   _____   _____

COMMENTS: _____

_____

Were there areas of discussion that
were not openly addressed?   YES _____   NO _____

If so, what? _____

_____

_____

_____

Would you like to see more meetings of
this type in the future?   YES _____   NO _____

General comments on the meeting: _____

_____

_____

_____

PLEASE RATE THIS MEETING ON THE SCALE BELOW. CIRCLE THE APPROPRIATE NUMBER:

| 1 (Poor) | 2 | 3 | 4 | 5 (Excellent) |

YOU MAY SUBMIT THIS ANONYMOUSLY AND USE BACK OF FORM FOR ADDITIONAL RESPONSES.

Source: Courtesy of Merck & Company

improve employee relations and productivity. It would be a mistake to assume that open communication means agreement. People can communicate openly and still disagree. The key objective is not 100 percent agreement but understanding each other's viewpoint.

PHYSICAL ARRANGEMENTS

Two-way communication is essential to these meetings and is most easily accomplished in a relaxed atmosphere. Small rooms are preferable, but large, more formal rooms can be satisfactory provided you make certain arrangements, for example, having participants sit close together in the front of the room. This arrangement can be achieved by a variety of means, including walling off the back part of the room and encouraging everyone to sit up front. To enhance informality Merck also recommends that you position yourself close to the audience and avoid using a stage if one is present. Merck believes if you think the meeting will last only 90 minutes or so, refreshments should be available before the meeting starts rather than during the meeting. Longer meetings usually work best if there is a refreshment break midway through the program.

For Face-to-Face meetings, smaller groups of 50 or fewer are best. Try to avoid filling an entire room by holding one mass meeting. If you are in charge of a large organization, more meaningful and candid conversation will occur if you divide large groups into small ones and hold more than one session. Merck believes it is not necessary to hold these small communication meetings on the same day or even close together. It has these communication meetings three or four times a year throughout the company. Face-to-Face meetings last about one and one-half to two hours. During these meetings, situate yourself at the head of the room with a lecture or table to hold your notes. Make a point of remaining visible to all participants.

Seating participants at small tables holding five to eight people helps maintain the informal and relaxed atmosphere so essential to a good meeting. Using tables is also advisable because there is room for taking notes and having refreshments. Merck has made use of large horseshoe-shaped tables with people sitting on the outside edges. If using a horseshoe table, stand at the open end. Merck says standing is better than sitting, because sitting gives the meeting too much of a formal appearance.

If there are windows in the meeting room, set it up so those attending are not looking out the windows. Draw the draperies if there is a risk of participants' becoming distracted. If charts, slides, overheads, or other audiovisuals are used, make sure they are readable to everyone in the audience. If a screen is needed, find out where to set up the projector and make sure you or someone else knows how to operate it. Finally, physical arrangements for the meeting should include providing participants with a copy of the meeting agenda, a list of presubmitted topics, evaluation forms, notepads, pencils, and name tags, if needed.

FOLLOW-UP

As already noted, it is wise to prepare evaluation forms and distribute them to participants at the end of the meeting. Later these evaluations will be tabulated and analyzed so potential trouble spots can be identified. Participants should be sent responses to any presubmitted requests that were not addressed in the meeting.

Within one week of the Face-to-Face meeting, Merck sends all participants a memo acknowledging their participation. At this time, it is wise to reemphasize your desire to increase open communication. The memo might also be used to refer to any presubmitted subjects that were not addressed or resolved at the meeting.

After the meeting, you should prepare your own summary of its results. Outline major topics discussed, including issues and concerns of top management, as well as your personal evaluation of the meeting's effectiveness. Then copies of this summary should be sent to your manager. Merck uses these summaries and evaluations to help senior management keep informed of the concerns of employees. A suggested sequence of events before and after the Face-to-Face meeting is seen in Figure 15.5.

COMMUNICATION SKILLS

Figure 15.5 shows some of the planning considerations for Face-to-Face meetings. Additionally, Merck has found out that there are several communication skills needed for effective meetings. When the meeting starts, normally you would welcome attendees, state the reason for the meeting, and review the agenda. At this point, it is probably a good idea to ask for questions about the agenda.

Once these concerns have been addressed, present your specific topic to the group. After each major point, be sure to pause and ask questions to test the group's understanding. Be sure to ask questions that must be answered with more than a "yes" or "no" statement. Proposing hypothetical situations and asking for a response to them can open up communication.

As you present your major points, pause at the end of each key point. You can wait for an answer to a question you have asked or for the group to respond to your hypothetical situation. If you still do not receive a response from the group, then repeat the question, either verbatim or

Figure 15.5
Countdown Checklist

Three to four weeks before the meeting:

- *Set date and time*

- *Reserve location for meeting*

- *Prepare list of participants*

- *Mail invitations and forms for pre-submitted questions and topics*

- *Order refreshments, if desired*

- *Arrange for audio-visual material and/or signs, if required*

Two weeks before the meeting:

- *Prepare agenda, 15, to 30, minute presentation or talk, and topics*

- *Confirm arrangements for meeting room and refreshments*

Day before the meeting:

- *Get supplies ready: agendas, lists of topics, evaluation forms, sharpened pencils, pads, etc.*

Day of the meeting:

- *Take supplies to the meeting room at least one hour before scheduled start*

- *Check that refreshments are ready*

- *Check that agenda, list of topics, pads and pencils, and evaluation forms are at each place setting.*

Within one week of the meeting:

- *Tabulate and analyze participant evaluations*

- *Prepare and send out copies of manager's summary*

- *Send out follow-up memo*

Source: Courtesy of Merck & Company

paraphrased. After all major points have been covered at the end of the presentation, ask for opinions about the information that was presented. If none is offered, then offer several possible opinions or suggestions and ask the entire group to respond to them.

During Face-to-Face meetings, responding skills are very important. The first of these skills is active listening. When you are asked a question, summarize it. Summary statements might include remarks like, "If I understand you, you are saying. . . ." or "I believe you are asking. . . ."

When asked a question, you can verify it or respond to it. If you want to verify a statement, you might say, "Is that right?" There are other equally verifying remarks. Assuming you know the answer to a question, you might want to respond by simply answering the question. If you do not know the answer, then say so. Then make a promise to get back to the questioner after the meeting.

Remember, if the subject matter of a question is extremely sensitive and you know the answer but cannot reveal it, say something like, "I'm sorry, but because of its confidential nature, I cannot discuss that at this time." If possible, let those asking the question know the reason for the silence or possible negative impact of revealing the information.

A common problem of many meetings is rambling by one or more participants at great length, which, if allowed to continue, can have a very negative impact. If someone is rambling, try to interrupt with a summary statement like, "Excuse me, but if I understand you, you are saying. . . ." or "Now what you are saying is. . . ."

In such meetings, there is also the risk that some people will wander off the subject. Merck refers to these wanderings as tangents. It tries to table the tangent remarks with a statement like, "Well, I understand your concern about that, but first let's decide. . . ." Another statement that has worked well is: "Let's come back to that point later. First we need to. . . ."

For meetings to be most successful, you must be able to give and receive criticism. This process is an art that must be practiced to be most effective. Rather than having a negative reaction to criticism, you can do several positive things. A positive way of handling criticism is either to summarize the remark or simply to verify it with a statement like, "Is that right?" Obviously, there is a variety of ways this statement could be said; there are many nonverbal clues that betray your true emotion.

When dealing with criticism, you must remain objective and not get your ego involved. Asking the person criticizing you or your idea why the concern was raised shows you are trying to be objective. A statement like, "Why do you think this is a problem?" goes a long way toward building trust. Likewise, when you have heard the criticism, do not overreact by saying something like, "You're wrong!" Merck has found that explaining the rationale behind the action defuses much of the criticism (*A Manager's*). Finally, be sure to thank the person for his or her "constructive" criticism—unless, of course, you do not want anyone else's criticism and want to defeat the purpose of Face-to-Face communication meetings.

Giving criticism, as well as receiving it, is another communication skill that must be learned. Some find it even harder to give it than receive it, but it is a skill that is going to be needed. When someone makes a suggestion that is difficult or impossible to implement, then giving criticism will be needed. It should always be aimed at the idea, not the person. If possible, try to isolate the merit of the idea while showing other consequences. Something like, "I understand why you are making that point, but there are some other things to consider, including. . . ." might be used (*A Manager's*). Another way of handling criticism is to ask for or offer suggestions on how to retain the merits of an idea and overcome the concerns of an individual or individuals. You can state the necessity of a certain action but ask for suggestions on how to overcome inherent problems with the approach.

Once the meeting is over, be sure to get back to individuals who had questions that could not be resolved with specific answers. Send follow-up memos and use your evaluation forms to help you plan your next meeting.

CONCLUDING THOUGHTS

Face-to-Face meetings serve a valuable purpose. They open up communication between and within levels of the organization. They provide managers and employees with an opportunity to discuss mutual concerns and, in the process, understand each other better. Face-to-Face meetings not only improve relations but also help employees do their jobs better, because they are provided with the information they need to do a better job. From a manager's standpoint, it is easier to lead if you understand the people you are supposed to be leading.

Merck has provided a shining example of how to plan and run Face-to-Face meetings. It suggests four rules: always be candid, be well prepared, encourage participation, and focus on listening. There are both procedural activities and human relations skills needed to run Face-to-Face meetings. Making use of pre-submitted questions, cross-functional, and multilevel groups enhances the effectiveness of this tool. Being able to address the tough issues and handling the normal rambling, going off on tangents, and criticism all require communication skills. Practicing your ability to summarize, paraphrase, and verify is just as essential as being well organized and prepared.

REFERENCES

A Manager's Guide to Face-to-Face Communication Meetings (booklet published by
     Merck & Co.).
Rice, Faye. "Champions of Communications." *Fortune*, June 3, 1991, 111–20.

16

Recognition

At the heart of a company's ability to be able to retain good employees is its ability to properly recognize and compensate people. There are many ways to do this, but in the end both effective recognition and compensation depend on a fundamental respect for the individual.

Thomas Watson, Jr., former CEO of IBM, was discussing the same type of respect when he was explaining the key to IBM's philosophy that led to its success; the most important part of that philosophy was "our respect for the individual" (Watson, 1963, 13). Watson said that it was a simple concept but that it occupies a major portion of management's time. That is the reason that IBM still places great emphasis on job security and on developing employees from within rather than hiring from the outside. Despite recessions there are no layoffs.

IBM was one of the first with a true open-door policy. It also was one of the first to begin eliminating barrier status that separates management and nonmanagement. For a long time, benefits have been the same for both groups. Everyone has been on a salary since 1958, when the company first eliminated hourly wages.

"THE HP WAY"

The central theme is fairness and equity. When it comes to recognition and compensation, there must be equity. Most great companies have this basic respect for the individual and need to treat them fairly. Listen to Dean Morton, chief operating officer for Hewlett-Packard (HP), and you can get a sense for what he thinks is critical to the company's success. He says, "HP's success depends upon our people, and therefore, it makes sense for us to show appreciation and recognition for those who have made our success possible" ("The Secret" 1987, 11).

He further emphasizes that HP has always relied on both the individual and teamwork and that management's job is to increase the visibility of individual and team contributions to its success. As a member of its functional management team, he encourages human resource managers to play a strategic role and take the initiative to influence their local area's employee motivational efforts. In his words, human resource has the opportunity to take a leadership role.

Morton believes that HP's quality and productivity gains will continue through its Total Quality Management (TQM) efforts and that TQM depends on motivated employees. In a competitive environment, employee motivation is essential but sometimes difficult to achieve. For large organizations like HP, employee motivation and recognition can be especially difficult. When you have 82,000 employees located in 77 countries, as HP does, companies can tend to become impersonal and bureaucratic. In small organizations it is easier to feel a sense of affiliation. In large ones, most people can get lost in the shuffle.

Morton notes that HP hears complaints from some of its employees that they are not being recognized for their contributions and that they never see enough of their managers. Some employees also say that their managers do not understand what they do and that they themselves do not always have a grasp of the "big picture" ("The Secret" 1987).

HP is generally recognized as an extremely well-run company. If some of its employees are expressing these concerns, chances are they are fairly widespread throughout most companies. Good communication is essential if employees are to feel they are appreciated and recognized.

FOUR KEY STRATEGIES

HP uses four key strategies that help give employees a sense of recognition and a feeling of contribution. Probably its most famous form of recognition comes through its Management-by-Wandering Around (MBWA), which is more than simply walking around and talking to people. It requires that managers keep up-to-date on employees and their activities through both informal and structured communication. It means a manager should reserve time to walk through a department as well as be consistently available for impromptu discussions. Discussion can take the form of coffee talks, communication lunches, and hallway conversations. Most importantly, MBWA requires that managers ask really good open-ended questions and that they know how to listen, to what they want to hear but to what is and is not being said.

Second, HP makes good use of Management-by-Objectives (MBO) as a recognition tool. The idea of MBO is for individuals to contribute to their company's goals by developing their own objectives, which, hopefully, fit within managerial and corporate goals. MBO provides a written plan that can be used to trace objectives through the organization. The goal of MBO at HP is to coordinate and integrate implementation efforts.

The third strategy HP uses to recognize the importance of employees is its Open Door policy, which, like MBO, is not new. Many, maybe even most, managers say they have open-door policies toward employees. With a true open-door policy, as in HP's case, employees must have 100 percent assurance that no adverse or negative consequences will occur because they raised an issue with management. As HP emphasizes, trust and integrity are an essential part of any open-door policy. When Open Door works, each party gets a clearer understanding of what is going on. HP uses it to discuss career options, proper business conduct, and communication breakdowns.

GOLD STARS

Activities like Open Door, MBO, and MBWA are not the only ways of recognizing the importance of your people. HP, along with most other firms, has awards that can be given for exceptional service. HP has a wide array of special awards. One of its divisions in Stanford Park gives an award called the Gold Star Program, which recognizes outstanding contributions by individuals.

HP's Colorado Springs division builds upon its MBWA philosophy by also giving a "Coin of the Realm." It is designed, like the Gold Star Program, to recognize achievements by employees in their division. It provides the general manager with a purposeful way to wander around the division and reward people. A committee elects recipients of the "coin" (which is actually a token), which can be redeemed for a free lunch in the cafeteria. At HP's Canada operation, there is a 100 percent club for all sales representatives who meet or exceed their quotas. The club uses occasional dinners and other forms of recognition.

Of all of the national and divisional awards that HP uses, perhaps one of the most interesting and creative was developed by Ron Gedris. He was the communication manager for the Pacific Technology Park operation. He developed an employee motivation/recognition wheel for managers at his site. The outer part of the wheel outlines types of activities deserving recognition, including such things as success with the Total Quality Control process, productivity improvements, meeting deadlines, and so on. The inner part of the wheel suggests of recognition, including employee photos on bulletin boards, reserved parking spaces near building entrances, and announcements of significant accomplishments at meetings or in company literature.

By spinning the inner wheel, one can align different combinations of activities and recognition methods. Gedris said he wanted a visual reminder of the importance of recognition. It is eye-catching and attaches to a wall. The point is that it is easy to forget how important recognition is when you are caught up in day-to-day deadlines and schedules. It is important to have some vehicle to remind people of the importance of recognition. Awards and visual reminders can do so provided they are used within the proper context.

CULTURAL AWARDS

For all of their glitter, awards may or may not be successful at recognizing or motivating people. If they stand alone with little relation to a company's culture, then chances are they will not be effective. If they reflect the culture of the company and they are a natural outgrowth of an atmosphere of employee recognition, then they can be effective.

One company that makes its awards a part of its culture and something of great value is Federal Express, America's first service company that has received the Malcolm Baldridge Quality Award. The company believes in the value of awards for its people. Its awards are not an add-on; rather, they are an integral part of its culture.

One of the awards that it uses to recognize its own people is called the Golden Falcon Award Program, which is given to permanent employees who demonstrate exceptional service to their customers.

The award is highly valued by the customer-focused culture of Federal Express. Candidates for the award are usually nominated based on unsolicited customer letters citing their outstanding performance. Nominated candidates are reviewed by the Golden Falcon Committee, and the final selection is made by their chief operating officers. Winners are announced monthly through Federal Express company publications or through company video program and are awarded a Golden Falcon lapel pin and shares of Federal Express common stock.

Another one of Federal Express's highly valued awards is called its Bravo Zulu Voucher Program, noted in Chapter 5. The Bravo Zulu flag is used by the U.S. naval services and means "well done." Federal Express developed the award as a way of reminding employees of the importance of teamwork and cooperation to the success of its business. Employees receive special recognition for exemplary performance that goes above and beyond their normal job duties. The flexible award lets managers recognize extraordinary performance with both cash and noncash awards. Noncash awards may take the form of sporting event tickets, theater tickets, dinner for two, and so on.

CONTINUAL FEEDBACK

HP and Federal Express have made good use of awards, but perhaps no one has such an awesome collection of awards as American Express, which has over 100 programs just for measuring, recognizing, and rewarding people who take unusual care of their customers. In addition to those mentioned in Chapter 9, these special events include use of prizes, raffle tickets, awards, and dinners. One award recognizes operating units whose quality performance has reached 100 percent for two consecutive months or 99 percent for three consecutive months. The company even has a higher standard, called the Super Quality Club.

American Express recognizes a Quality Employee of the Month. This person is selected by departmental members and is chosen for outstanding quality achievements. On a quarterly basis, these individuals are awarded a special recognition lunch, certificates, and T-shirts.

Corporate quality assurance personnel also monitor telephone conversations, and when the detect extraordinary quality performance by employees, they send them a Quality Commendation. The award is sent not only to the individual but also to that person's boss and to all levels of management within his or her center. The commendation is also placed in that individual's personnel file.

Not all of American Express's recognition is in the form of awards; a great deal of the recognition effort is focused on communication. The company uses many forms, including something it calls Q-tips. These reports are used when its Quality Assurance people detect error patterns or quality problems that need to be communicated throughout the company. Q-tips are designed to be lighthearted ways of making people aware of these problems.

American Express also uses a Quality Hot Line, by which an individual within one of its centers can contact a specialist about how to handle specific customer inquiries.

The company also publishes weekly and monthly performance statistics, so people have feedback about their and others' performance. Individuals have even daily feedback through an on-line computer management information system. This system shows each manager every error for each day of the week. Using this system, each manager can see his or her employee's quality performance.

The company also periodically uses video camera crews who interview employees throughout a center and then display the results of those interviews on monitors strategically located throughout the building. One of the previous themes of these video interviews was "What Quality Means to Me." Employee recognition is also enhanced through a newsletter, *New Horizons*, which features other achievements and accomplishments each month as well as employees' photographs.

All of American Express's awards and communication tools and the awards of HP and Federal Express have one thing in common. This common theme was described by HP's John Cardon, who was the personnel manager of its Logic System Division in Colorado Springs. He was referring to a survey HP had conducted to find out what its employees wanted in a recognition program. What he discovered is probably fairly typical of all employees. In summarizing the results of the survey, he said that people just wanted their supervisors to communicate more regularly with them to know what they are doing and to appreciate the difficulty of their jobs.

THE HIGHEST FORM OF RECOGNITION

So far we have looked at a wide array of recognition awards and communication tools used by some outstanding companies. Awards and communication with employees can be beneficial because they let people know their work is appreciated. There is, however, a higher form of recognition.

The highest form of recognition you can give employees is changing your relationship with them. Improving relationships is more than simple awards. Real recognition of the importance of the employee comes when you change working relationships. This change is not easy to accomplish. It is easier simply to give someone an award than to change relationships. One company that seems to have been able to change relationships is American Airlines.

In its case the vehicle for changing relationships was its Quality of Work Life (QWL) activities, a different way of thinking and doing work so as to improve working relationships. The goal of QWL at American Airlines was to treat employees with dignity and respect and to encourage them to participate in its decision-making process.

Goals such as these are almost always only partially achieved, if at all. Even the best companies will struggle with any system that seeks greater employee participation and involvement. Anyone wishing to go from the "tell 'em and sell 'em" supervisor to subordinate approach to a more flexible colleague approach should not expect the change to be easy. Developing a partnership approach between management and nonmanagement has not been easy for American Airlines, but it is making headway.

Its QWL efforts began in 1984, with the objective to listen to what people said and, most importantly, understand what they meant. QWL at American Airlines meant greater sharing of responsibility and authority throughout the company. American Airlines management says that it believes most workplace problems should be solved from the bottom up instead of from the top down. The rationale is that usually the best solutions are developed by those who are closest to the problem. At American Airlines, QWL attempts to share the responsibility for both identifying problems and developing solutions to these problems.

To make QWL or other forms of real employee recognition work, they must be believable. Employee involvement and recognition must be thought of as a process that includes several ingredients. First of all, it takes real commitment to convince employees that you really do want their involvement. It means seeking their involvement before decisions are made or policies have been set. It means managers must always explain the reason decisions are made. Employees must know what and why something is happening.

To recognize the value of employees, use every opportunity and every means available to communicate. American Airlines uses meetings, written and electronic messages, newsletters, videos, and telephones to keep employees involved.

True changes in relations require new skills in how to work as a team and how to diagnose and solve problems. When American Airlines recognized the importance of the operational person, it knew that having a desire to participate was not enough. First, employees were taught how to work as a team and how to solve problems.

SUCCESS STORIES

So what did American Airlines get out of its QWL efforts? Rather than one thing, it achieved a series of success stories that allowed them to inch toward greater competitiveness. At JFK Airport flight attendants initiated an "Island Council" to solve problems related to food services and packing procedures for catering supplies. In Salt Lake City, a QWL group suggestion led to the formation of a special airport service called "ski patrol" in which skis are given to special check-in attendants to improve services.

A QWL group suggested a reservations system that created a "floating" holiday. This plan alone saved American Airlines an estimated $43,000 for just the President's Day holiday. The plan entails an employee's volunteering to work on a holiday in exchange for a day off of the agent's choice.

In Philadelphia, a QWL committee and local management collaborated to build an employee shower. The company provided the materials, and local employees contributed their time and effort. In another case, an American Airlines support services group spearheaded the formation of an advisory group to achieve safety and more efficient and less costly operations. The group ended up saving the company over $12 million by rebuilding equipment from spare parts and by implementing safety awareness programs that cut down equipment damages and repair costs. At the Dallas/Fort Worth Airport a QWL employee council established a privately owned and operated child care center, with the company's providing support and assistance.

Additionally, American Airlines mechanic crews at several airports have rebuilt or modified cabin service trucks, wreckers, equipment maintenance trucks, and other assorted vehicles at great savings for the company. This equipment, which was rebuilt from the ground up, cost American Airlines less to maintain and operate and is more efficient than original equipment.

At Denver, preelected representatives solicited design suggestions from all employees and participated in recommending features for the new terminal. At New York's JFK Airport, a "Take a Walk in My Shoes" program lets ticket agents and fleet service clerks switch places for a day so they can gain a better perspective of each other's job. In Indianapolis, QWL teams helped create more flexible work schedules. At the Dallas/ Fort Worth Airport, representatives from all five domestic divisions helped redesign their SABRE reservation system. In Tulsa, employees participated in the layout, design, and equipping of new work areas and in rewriting maintenance computer programs. In Philadelphia, QWL helped develop a better baggage-sorting system. In Amarillo, employees nominated other employees for recognition. The list of QWL improvements goes on and on.

Besides the savings from these QWL efforts, the real value of them is the meaningful change they create in relationships. Such changes cannot be completely or totally measured, but they add up to a real competitive advantage. This process of improving relations increases any program's chances of success.

At most corporations employee suggestion programs are a corporate joke, and few employees pay any attention to them. American Airlines implemented an employee suggestion system called "Innovation," which was systematic, not stingy, and most importantly, it demonstrated respect for the individual. In 12 weeks of operation it generated 1,550 ideas that were adopted by the company. The 535 teams participating won prizes worth $4.7 million, but the program saved the company more than $20 million in cost savings and revenue-generating ideas.

CONCLUDING THOUGHTS

Everyone needs recognition and appreciation, but they must be more than pats on the back, letters of appreciation, and awards for exceptional performance. Recognition needs to occur on a daily basis, as with Hewlett-Packard's Management-by-Wandering-Around.

This discussion about recognition began with Watson's comments. He said the heart of IBM's success was its respect for the individual, and for this reason it feels a need for equity in the workplace. There are no layoffs, and there are open doors and few barriers for management and nonmanagement alike.

In the end, though, the highest form of recognition comes with fundamental changes between these groups. Stories like American Airlines's QWL efforts are heartening because of what can be accomplished when employees are allowed to become partners. Creating a more participating environment, as at American Airlines, does not occur overnight and may never be totally achieved. It takes real, sincere commitment to use every means possible to communicate and to keep employees more involved in both big and small decisions. Most of all, it takes a commitment to respect their ability.

REFERENCES

"The Secret of Our Success." *Exchange* (Hewlett-Packard in-house publication), October-November 1987, 11.
Watson, Thomas J. *A Business and Its Beliefs*. New York: McGraw-Hill, 1963, 13.

17

Compensation

A friend of mine is a CEO of a very successful small business. He and his staff have a phrase they use: "Stop the Praise, Give Me a Raise." His point is not that motivation is not important; rather, you should recognize that money is, and probably always will be, a very important form of recognition. Granted, it is not the only thing people are interested in, but it is one of the keys to motivation.

The CEO who uses this phrase does not pay his employees more than competing companies, yet they work harder, stay longer, and turn out better quality than employees at his competitor's plants. The company is employee-owned and operated, but many of those types of companies have not been successful. The key to his success is the same as that for Watson when he was discussing the success of IBM: at his plant, there is a fundamental respect for the ability and intelligence of people.

The key point with compensation, as with recognition, is equity. Management has to be fair and open. My friend's plant has open disclosure of the company's assets, liabilities, and so on and put knowledge of how to make good decisions in the hands of the lowest personnel. Everyone understands a balance sheet and how to read an income statement. Employees decide whether to invest or increase bonuses. It is a financial and emotional partnership. Contrast this attitude with what is often occurring.

INEQUITY

Compensation, or rather the inequity in compensation, has become a very big and divisive issue. Consider the flap over executive pay. Many top executives are taking a lot of heat, sometimes for good reasons, over what many perceive as excessive compensation. The *Washington Post* reported that Thomas Spiegel, former head of Columbia Savings and Loan of Beverly Hills, California, allegedly squandered depositors' money on air travel, vacation homes, and rock concerts. David L. Paul headed the failed CenTrust Savings Bank of Miami and entertained politicians on a $7 million yacht at company expense. He used corporate funds to pay for a $13.2 million Rubens painting, which he hung in his living room. Armand Hammer, the late chairman of Occidental Petroleum Corporation, upset shareholders with plans to spend $150 million to build and endow an art museum to be named for him and to house his personal collections.

While such abuses are newsworthy, they are not the only inequity that has sensitized John Q. Public. The abuse of executive pay has also been receiving a lot of newsprint. In particular, the issue of executive pay and its relationship to both the pay of lowest-level employees and the overall performance of the company is of most concern. If employees lost faith and trust in higher officials, the company is in trouble. If they believe that there is great inequity, then the words of management will mean little. When the public, many of whom are employees, read a cover story by *Business Week* featuring abuses of executive pay, then you know the issue is becoming big ("The Flap" 1991). When they hear that executives like John Sculley, CEO of Apple Computer, made over $16 million or that Paul B. Firemane, CEO of Nike, made over $14 million, then you know employees are going to question their own executives' salaries.

What upsets most people is not so much that some executives can make enormous amounts of money; rather, it is the relationship among their pay, corporate performance, and perceived risks. *Business Week* reported that in the past decade CEO compensation jumped 212 percent, while factory workers saw their pay increase only 53 percent, engineers 73 percent, and teachers 95 percent. During this same time, the average earnings per share grew only by 78 percent ("The Flap" 1991). In 1990, as profits of companies slid by 7 percent, the average executive's salary and bonus rose by 3.5 percent to $1,214,090. If you add in gains from long-term compensation such as stock options, the average CEO's total pay climbed 7 percent to $1,952,806.

Peter Drucker expressed doubts about the pay for CEOs and suggested that a CEO should not earn more than 20 times as much as the company's lowest-paid employee ("The Flap" 1991) Last year the average chief executive of a major corporation made 85 times the pay of the typical factory worker. By contrast, in Japan the boss receives only 17 times the pay of ordinary workers ("The Flap" 1991). Plato, the Greek philosopher, would have the ratio for leaders of men to be even lower, at 5 to 1.

Plato's ratio will never happen within a modern corporation, but the current compensation inequity must be addressed before employees will believe they are all playing on the same team. Inequity is often at the heart of employee productivity and morale problems. Those same ideas were expressed by Graef S. Crystal, the so-called dean of compensation consultants ("The Flap" 1991). If Iacocca gets a 25 percent increase in pay and his company's earnings drop by 79 percent, then something must be wrong.

ALTERNATIVES

Compensation inequity is not the only reason compensation plans are being reconsidered. Flatter pyramids, labor shortages, and downsizing have meant rethinking traditional pay plans. One increasingly popular pay plan, whose time seems to have come, is dual-track compensation. The principle is simple: pay the best nonmanagerial professional on par with the managers.

One such plan has been implemented by Texas Instruments's (TI) Johnson City, Tennessee, operation. Kenneth V. Spenser, TI's vice president of its worldwide industrial control business, announced his plan while giving a speech to a gathering of Johnson City personnel. The facility was in the process of restructuring and eliminating managerial layers. By late 1989, it had trimmed managerial staff from 240 to 103. There were a few dismissals, but most of those displaced managers simply returned to the technical and engineering disciplines from which they had come (Sheridan 1990). The interesting part is they did so without sacrificing the chance for career advancement. Those displaced managers and others within the company could advance and receive greater equity through its "technical ladders."

The Johnson City operation is unique because its technical ladder allowed it to downsize and end up with a more efficient business, without a drop in morale. The key was its technical ladders. These ladders at TI are equal in status and pay to those in managerial areas. At Johnson City there are eight rungs to the ladder including associate engineer, engineer, senior engineer, master engineer, member of group technical staff, senior member of technical staff, fellow, and senior fellow. Spenser noted, "Senior fellow is a position right next to God" (Sheridan 1990, 53). Those at the top of the technical ladder can make as much as a vice president of the corporation.

MENUS

Dual-track compensation is an exciting alternative, but it cannot completely eliminate compensation inequity. In other cases, it simply is not appropriate. There is, however, no shortage of alternative ways of compensating employees. Typically a company can use a variety of plans. For instance, Hewlett-Packard (HP) has a very good, but not unusual, pay and benefit package that includes:

- cash profit-sharing program
- employee assistance program
- stock-purchase program
- flexible time off
- choice of health plans
- eleven paid holidays
- income protection plan
- educational assistance plan
- life insurance coverage
- comprehensive retirement benefit

It also has a protection bonus plan that essentially pays about 30 percent of sales to employees through a combination of wages, salaries, and bonus. With a sense of equity, this same percentage is paid to the janitor and top managers alike.

A PIECE OF THE ROCK

Brunswick's CEO, Jack Reichert, recognized the value of equity and wanted everyone to be a shareholder in the company. As early as 1983, Reichert won board approval to match contributions with additional shares paid out of the company's earnings. Today the net worth of the company's 26,000 employees is well over $45 million in Brunswick stock. As of 1988, if an employee had been in the plan for five years, he or she would have had about 120 shares. Brunswick believes stock gives people a feeling that they are working together for one single company. In the next chapter we will look at an even more radical option for compensating employees, including the use of stock options for everyone.

Stock options are not new. In 1958, HP instituted a small stock option plan using 100 shares for a job well done. In 1959, it established an employee stock purchase plan with a 25 percent subsidy from the company.

Federal Express, among others, also purchase shares of stock for all participants. An employee purchase price is 85 percent of the average market value on the first or last day of the quarterly period. Stock options, like many other compensation tools, have broadened. In the next chapter we will see how they have changed, including the PepsiCo stock option plan for all 100,000 workers. They are not just an executive compensation tool anymore, and that fact makes the workplace more equitable.

INCENTIVE PROGRAMS

Money not only talks but also motivates, according to an industrial engineering survey ("P & Q" 1990). No surprise here, but the survey did make one point clear. Industrial engineers were asked, If employees' pay was linked to their performance, would their company's productivity increase? A resounding 85 percent of those surveyed agreed that a financial reward is a major factor in increasing a company's productivity. Furthermore, 75 percent of respondents said employee incentive programs were important to a company's success ("P & Q" 1990). There are many kinds of these programs.

Gain Sharing

One of the most popular and effective worker incentive plans being used today is gain sharing. Essentially, these plans set up some reward for employees that improves corporate quality, productivity, or customer service goals. Usually when a person or department is able to beat predetermined performance targets, all members receive bonuses.

Gain sharing requires measurable objectives and employee involvement. On the plus side, these plans improve teamwork and cooperation as employees learn to focus on bonus objectives. The risk of such plans is that they focus only on productivity and ignore other criteria; therefore, goals have to be carefully framed. The risk from the company's perspective is that these bonuses may have to be paid even if the company is unprofitable.

Many feel gain sharing is worth the risk because it is a powerful motivator. Its power rests with the fact that it directly connects pay to performance. It rewards people for results they can directly influence (e.g., making more circuit boards per hour, serving more accounts, and so on). One of the most popular forms of gain-sharing is IMPROSHARE, created by Mitchell Fein.

Fortune magazine noted that in 1986 Carrier needed 118 man-hours to get a finished product out the door. Using IMPROSHARE, workers produced more, acceptable good products per hour. The resulting savings, under a gain-sharing plan like Improshare, are split 50/50. Everyone from maintenance employees to managers gains the same percentage bonus. At Carrier plants, productivity information is posted daily on bulletin boards, and employees are encouraged to tell management about their ideas.

Fein provides an example of how his plan works. Suppose in a year's time a plant generates 200,000 hours of work and produces 50,000 units, the average time per unit is four hours per unit. That is your baseline. Now suppose in one week workers work faster and produce 1,300 units in 4,080 hours. If you take the 1,300 units and multiply them by the standard of four hours per unit, it should have taken employees 5,200 hours to produce their product. However, since they were motivated, they produced the product in 4,080 hours, not 5,200, and saved 1,120 hours. With Improshare's 50/50 split you would take the employee's half of the 1,120, or 560, and divide it by the total hours worked, or 4,080, the result is 13.7 percent additional pay that each employee would receive (Fein 1991). Both management and employees gain from the productivity increases.

The company gains not only increased productivity but also a more committed work force. Take the case of Carrier. When a water main broke at one of its facilities, several machines fell into a sinkhole. Employees labored day and night to get the machines up and running so they would not miss their weekly bonus (Perry 1988).

For this plan to work, Fein says management must be willing to share and listen (Perry 1988). At Carrier, the plan seems to be working for both management and employees. So far its 2,500 employees have received over $3 million in bonuses, and management has received a far more committed work force.

Lump-Sum Bonus

Lump-sum bonus incentives, along with gain-sharing plans, have become increasingly popular. Lump-sum bonuses involve employees' receiving a onetime cash payment based on performance. Such a payment does not go into one's base pay. For this incentive to be effective, the plan must be fair and management must have a good relationship with employees. From a managerial standpoint, its main advantage is that the plan helps control fixed costs by limiting pay raises and benefits. A sometimes serious drawback is that award bonuses can sometimes be seen as subjective and therefore unfair.

Pay-for-Knowledge

Some of the newer incentive plans compensate based on Pay-for-Knowledge. With a Pay-for-Knowledge incentive, an employer's salary rises with the number of tasks he or she can do, regardless of the job performed. It requires that management identify the skills that must be mastered and that human resources develop assessment and training procedures.

The value of this incentive is that it greatly increases a company's flexibility and allows you to operate with a leaner staff. It also provides employees with a broader perspective since they do more than one task. On the downside, labor costs will generally be higher because more employees will learn more applicable skills. Training costs also tend to increase.

Pay-for-Knowledge incentives, like these used by Rohn and Haas Bayport, have grown in direct proportion to the explosion of team management concepts. Multi-skilled teams are all the rage, and one of the best ways to get them is to encourage team members to broaden their skills. Chaparral Steel operates one of the world's most productive steel companies, and team management is a big part of its success.

Earl Englehart, who runs its educational program, teaches mill hands both what happens to a piece of steel and the roles of finance, accounting, and sales. The objective is to teach workers how each job relates to every other. Chaparral Steel, like many companies that use team management, uses a pay-for-skill incentive, rather than traditional flat salary and automatic raises. Pay is based on what an employee has learned, not on seniority. For instance, if a steelworker learns how to run a new piece of equipment, he or she might get a 5 percent raise (Dumaine 1990). Generally, younger employees like this system, while more experienced employees do not like it.

PROFIT SHARING

Profit sharing is a more established incentive program. It is used by about 30 percent of all U.S. companies. In essence, employees receive an annual bonus that varies, based on corporate profits. Payment is made in cash or deferred into retirement plans. For profit sharing to work, employees must believe they can collectively influence corporate profit. Owners must also value their employees' contributions to profit. The plan is easy to implement and to communicate, and it is affordable since you pay only if it is profitable.

A serious drawback to many such plans is that when you focus on annual payments, people tend to ignore long-term performance and improvements. Likewise, employees must clearly see that they can control and influence profit and that it is not an entitlement program. This is a key point of any effective incentive plan.

VARIABLE PAY

In a survey by the Public Agenda Foundation of 845 blue- and white-collar workers, approximately 45 percent believed there is no link between pay and performance (Dumaine 1990). They are right! Often profit sharing or merit raises have little to do with who deserves it. Union contracts often require that everyone get a raise.

The point is that if everyone gets it, it is not an incentive. Almost everyone knows people need incentives, but creating effective ones is another matter. Jude Rich, president of Sibson & Co., a human resource consulting firm, says the United States spends $125 billion on employee incentives, but experts say roughly half of those incentive plans do not work. One that does is at Lincoln Electric.

Lincoln Electric in Cleveland pays workers on a piecemeal basis. For each acceptable piece they produce, employees receive a certain number of dollars. Each worker then receives a yearly merit rating based on things like dependability, ideas generated, quality, and output, which serve as the basis for year-end bonuses that average 97.6 percent of regular earnings (Perry 1988). This incentive plan is one of the reasons that Lincoln has had 54 years without a losing quarter and, according to one study, has workers who are up to three times as productive as their counterparts in similar manufacturing.

Variability in pay is an essential feature in the success of the Lincoln plan and is missing in most U.S. pay plans. According to one report, Japanese workers receive an average of 25 percent of total pay in the form of flexible bonuses. In contrast, American firms average around 1 percent (Perry 1988). In the same article, economist Martin Weitzman of MIT states that such variable pay, if used nationwide, could ease inflation and reduce unemployment since companies would be more likely to hire more and fire less. He thinks 20 percent of the total compensation in the United States should be variable.

AT RISK

In addition to variability, other effective pay incentives have a certain amount of risk associated with them. Consider the approach that CRAY Research uses. It has an annual incentive award that is designed to recognize and reward key employees for significant contributions. The plan supplements existing base salary and profit sharing for experienced engineers, administrators, and managers. One unique feature is that the proportion of pay put at risk diminishes with diminishing rank. The higher in rank you are, the more at risk your pay becomes. A central operating officer, for example, would be allowed to fall to 76 percent of the reference average for all executives of similar rank. A software engineer, on the other hand, could fall only to 96 percent (Aguilan 1990).

DuPont's fiber division has its own plan, which involves contributing part of its annual wage and salary increase into an "at-risk pot." Six percent of employees' annual pay is put into company's bonus plan, which is based on how close the division comes to annual target earnings. As with any at-risk plan, there is a downside. If the division does not meet at least 80 percent of its objectives, employees lose everything they put into the pot. Criticism of this plan has been that employees who work in a department have little control over the results.

Perhaps one of the best at-risk pay plans is used by Nucor, a $1 billion a year nonunion steelmaker. While workers earn wages only half those of their union counterparts, their bonuses average well over 100 percent of that base. As a result, workers earn $32,000 or roughly $2,000 more than their union counterparts.

If workers are late, they lose their bonus for the day. Workers who are more than 30 minutes late lose their bonuses for the whole week (Perry 1988). Departmental managers earn a bonus on return on plant assets. Plant managers receive a bonus on overall return on equity. At the end of the year, the company distributes 10 percent of pre-tax earnings to all employees.

MANAGERIAL CONSIDERATIONS

So far we have looked at a variety of innovative compensation plans. Each has its own merits and drawbacks. One common feature of all of these plans, and of any other plan, is that for them to work, employees must understand the connection between compensation and performance. Many compensation plans that work in theory do not work because management has not made this connection clear. Making the plans work will require a great deal of training and communication. Both will be needed to help employees understand the compensation system and why they should support it. Innovative pay plans can improve employees' perception of the company, but not unless the benefits of the plans are explained and fear is alleviated.

Communication and training of employees are essential to a pay plan's success, but they alone will not ensure its success. Many human resource compensation plans often fail fully to involve managers and supervisors in the process so they are knowledgeable about them. Unless supervisors and managers understand and support a pay plan, no innovative approach to pay will work. After all, they will be the ones who explain pay ranges and appraisals. If the new compensation system results in eliminating employees' cost of living or lowers the salary scale, then supervisors must be able to explain why these changes are good.

Understanding is essential. Before a compensation plan is introduced, try to make every effort to determine both employee and supervisory attitudes toward pay. To develop a sound compensation strategy, set reasonable objectives by analyzing employee perceptions. Use surveys, individual discussions, interviews, and any other means available to get a better understanding of current attitudes.

Once you understand current attitudes, you can then develop a compensation strategy that meets employees' needs. Choosing a particular compensation plan depends on their attitudes, your needs, the price of jobs in the marketplace, and how closely you want to link pay to performance.

Employees will have plenty of questions. Human resource managers must have answers to those questions if there is any hope of creating a positive climate. Typically employees will want to know how they will be paid and how the new pay plan will affect their current pay. You will have to explain what raises are based on and why. Most importantly, you will need to show employees that their performance really does matter. Most of them probably believe, as the earlier survey noted, that there is little connection between pay and performance and that you get paid the same no matter how hard you work.

CONCLUDING THOUGHTS

These plans are not the only ways to compensate people; there are many other unique ways. For instance, Federal Express's policy of promotion from within, rather than hiring from the outside, could be thought of as a compensation plan. Generally, though, most of the highly successful compensation plans have two things in common: they link pay to performance, and they put greater pay at risk. In reference to earlier remarks about CEOs' pay, many think companies have a lot of nerve since many executives' pay is unrelated to profits. Notwithstanding normal cynicism, dynamic incentives are increasingly popular.

Part of the reason there has been a shift in variable, more dynamic pay is that America has become a service economy. Since labor costs can use up to 60 to 70 percent of a service's total operating budget, variable pay plans are increasingly popular. Such incentive plans are being used in hospitals, banks, and other services.

Incentives are popular for another reason. When you closely tie performance to pay, you get greater productivity, which in turn holds down wages and wage-related benefits. Such factors are essential during increased competitive pressures.

REFERENCES

Aguilar, Francis J. "CRAY Research: Preparing for the 1990s." *Harvard Business School Case Studies*, January 17, 1990, 8.

Dumaine, Brian. "Who Needs a Boss?" *Fortune*, May 7, 1990, 58.

Fein, Mitchell. *IMPROSHARE: An Alternative to Traditional Managing*. Norcross, GA: Mitchell Fein Institute of Industrial Engineering, 1991, 43.

"The Flap over Executive Pay." *Business Week*, May 6, 1991, 90–93.

"P & Q Survey." *Focus. Industrial Engineering*. May 1990, 6.

Perry, Nancy J. "Here Come Richer, Riskier Pay Plans." *Fortune*, December 19, 1988, 51–58.

Sheridan, John H. "Lean But Not Mean." *Business Week*, February 19, 1990, 53.

18

Entrepreneurial Spirit

A great deal of managerial discussion in this book has centered on the need to empower employees and give them a sense of ownership and pride in their work. Options have included flattening organizational pyramids and using team management. Profit sharing and employee stock option plans (ESOPs) have all been used with varying degrees of success.

The common denominator, which many companies are seeking and a few achieve, is the need to create an entrepreneurial spirit within the company. Such a spirit is a sense that one is working for oneself rather than just for someone else. Those with an entrepreneurial spirit feel they have a stake in the business and can directly affect the success of that business.

Doubtless, some people within just about every organization have this entrepreneurial spirit. Certain CEOs, vice presidents, and other "critical" players often get a sense that the business is theirs. The trouble is that not enough people have this sense of ownership. While a few can lead, all must participate if organizations are to run effectively. If it were possible somehow to empower all of the work force with this entrepreneurial spirit, think what could be possible! We would have everyone who thought like managers and acted like owners; we would have organizations that could compete with anyone. There would be less strife, more cooperation. If everyone cared as much as we do, or cared more, then work would be a more enjoyable activity.

In this last chapter we will look at two companies that have made grand experiments in this area and that could not be more different from each other. The first is PepsiCo, Inc., which is the giant corporation that owns Kentucky Fried Chicken (KFC), Pizza Hut, and Taco Bell. It has begun an innovative journey it hopes will instill this entrepreneurial spirit, through a stock option program it calls "SharePower."

Leaders can innovate, but people must act. Large organizations have a great deal of inertia, and it takes greater efforts to make course corrections, but at least PepsiCo's management has steered in the right direction with SharePower. It holds enormous potential.

While PepsiCo's journey is just beginning, the second company is further along the path toward entrepreneurialism. Springfield Remanufacturing Corporation (SRC) is a small (600 employees) company that rebuilds engines and engine components. It has been tremendously successful and the focus of numerous articles, a television special, "Growing Your Business," and at least two books. The focus of attention is its approach toward employee involvement, sharing of information, and the entrepreneurial spirit that it is able to create among even the lowest-level employees. Like any great effort, it is not a program; it is a process, and the company's efforts are constantly changing and transforming. In a moment, we will look at some of the most exciting and most recent transformations, but first let's look at PepsiCo's innovative approach.

SHAREPOWER

In the true spirit of entrepreneurialism, SharePower is an effort to spread decision making to lower levels, create a greater sense of team spirit, and make it easier for employees to identify with the company and their work. Upper management also hoped employees would stay longer and increase their productivity. With these goals in mind, SharePower was created.

What is so unique about a stock option plan? After all, stock option plans have been around for years. As the name implies, stock options give you the option of purchasing stock through some deferred program. In the past, they have been quite a status symbol. Many still see stock options as the ultimate symbol of having made it, and for good reason. Typically options are offered only to a company's top executives. At one time only the top 100 or so executives of a large corporation would be rewarded with the opportunity to purchase stock options. Many large organizations still operate that way, but recently these options have been offered to a wider range of a company's top 300 or 400 executives. So what is PepsiCo's difference? Simply that it offers options to all 100,000 employees who work an average of at least 30 hours a week. Everyone from truck drivers to taco makers can participate.

BACKGROUND

PepsiCo's reason for creating SharePower was to have everyone feel the sense of ownership that top executives felt. SharePower began when Wayne Calloway, chairman and CEO of PepsiCo, challenged the personnel staff to come up with an idea that would "spread employee empowerment and ownership" to every level of the organization ("PepsiCo" 1989). He wanted a motivator that would reward longer service and be good for all shareholders.

Over the next two years the personnel department looked at several programs, but none of them seemed to be satisfactory for the company's needs. Some seemed to be simply savings programs and did not provide incentives. Many such programs required employees to set aside funds in order to benefit from the program. At best about two-thirds of employees actually participated in such programs. PepsiCo wanted a program for all employees. It looked at various ESOPs, but management felt these were primarily entitlement programs and not motivational; furthermore, ESOPs did not reward long service.

The idea of stock options for everyone in the corporation came to Charlie Rogers, the vice-president of compensation and benefits, in the fall of 1988, while he was waiting at a traffic light. He knew stock options were reserved for a select few, but he could not think why options could not work for everyone. When he got back to his office, he assigned a benefits team to check out the possibility. Within months, a stock program called SharePower was developed. In March 1989, PepsiCo's Board of Directors approved the program. PepsiCo acquired the stock from the open market by borrowing funds; this move caused little or no dilution, and the company feels any dilution is outweighed by the stock price's gain over time.

HOW DOES IT WORK?

Under ideal conditions an employee earning $30,000 can make more than $387,000 over a 30-year career, if stock prices increase 10 percent annually, an increase that is not unexpected. PepsiCo's stock price has increased at an annual average compound rate of 11.2 percent since its formation in 1965 to June 1989. If the stock prices were to grow at an annual rate of 15 percent, the same person earning $30,000 a year would make not $387,000, but $1.2 million.

Under the plan, each July 1, employees who work 30 hours a week and 1,000 hours a year are granted options totaling 10 percent of their compensation, including bonuses, overtime, and other extras for the previous year (Solomon 1989). The value of these options on July 1 will be equal to 10 percent of the employee's cash earnings. Options give employees the right to buy company stock at the July 1 price anytime within the next ten years. Since options let employees purchase shares of stocks at the July 1 price, they can profit from their efforts to make the company more profitable. Employees can exercise each annual grant at 20 percent per year. They do not have to have the cash in hand to make the purchase and can use the appreciation in stock value over time to buy stock (Solomon 1989).

Like all stocks, PepsiCo's price fluctuates daily, and it is possible that the price of its stock might not increase; it could even fall. If that happens, employees—like stockholders—will not make a profit, but they will not lose anything. PepsiCo management emphasizes to its employees that the amount employees receive will depend on everyone's ability to increase the value of his or her stock and on how long each employee is willing to let the stock grow before selling it. Employees do not have to do anything to participate except continue to work for the company for at least one year. This time allows the grants to be exercisable. As noted before, each year's grant vests at 20 percent per year; after five years, grants are fully vested.

PepsiCo's stock option plan has received very positive comments; however, there is a warning. Compensation experts warn others who might consider following PepsiCo's lead with stock options to make sure they are simply one part of an overall empowerment plan. Michael Halloran, vice president of the consulting firm Towers Perrin, says that the plan will not work unless top management is pushing teamwork (Solomon 1989). It is essential that options be part of the package, not the whole package. Such a stock option package cannot grow unless it occurs within a participative and open environment where equity, not inequity, is the foundation of the company.

CREATING A BUSINESS

One of the most dynamic ways of creating equity is to help employees create their own company within the company, as was mentioned in Chapter 6. After two years as a Hyatt switchboard operator and assistant housekeeping manager, John Allegetti was ready to quit. He hated the long wait for promotions. He hated the repetition of his job, and he realized the hotel business wasn't for him. He wanted a more challenging job. He wanted to help the environment, but, after a month of sending around his resume and interviewing waste-recycling facilities, he ended up back at Hyatt doing what he wanted to do.

Allegetti's boss, believing he showed promise and not wanting to lose him, asked Allegetti to head a project to reduce waste at the 2,000-room hotel. Allegetti did such a good job that the parent Hyatt corporation let him develop and run a new waste-consulting business called International ReCycle Co., Inc. As noted earlier, this company not only has several large Hyatt customers but also has 24 clients in eight states (Ellis 1990).

The Chicago Hyatt's goal of keeping people hyped has become a way of life for this flagship hotel. Since aspiring hoteliers must wait to run a small hotel, the company continues to expand its motivational efforts. Now, the Chicago Hyatt is helping employees with novel ideas outside the company's core business to set up free-standing companies. In three years, employee suggestions have prompted Hyatt to spin off a half dozen ventures in such things as party catering, retirement apartment complexes, and sporting equipment rental shops (Ellis 1990).

Like Allegetti, those who develop the ideas are usually the ones allowed to run them. As noted earlier, they receive start-up capital but do not get an equity stake. Hyatt sets up the ventures as separate companies and lets its corporate staff keep its focus on hotels.

James E. Jones was director of the sales development for Hyatt. He noticed that party planners were receiving hefty fees for some of the same services Hyatt could provide. Because of his work at the hotel, he had wide contact with professional sports, a big source for event planners. He knew Hyatt could do this work, and if it did not want to do it, he was ready to quit and do it himself. He made up a business plan, sold the idea to Hyatt Hotels president, Darryl Hartley-Leonard, and was given $780,000 start-up money. Through the new company, Hyatt's party planner, called Regency Productions, secured a contract from the National Football League, the 1991 Super Bowl, and 1991 U.S. Open golf tournament.

There are problems, of course, in helping employees set up a company within their company. Often proposals are made by employees who lack financial skills. In Jones's case, he was weak on contingency planning. The company sent him back to solidify the proposal rather than rejecting it outright.

EQUALITY IS EQUITY

One company that has this emphasis on teamwork and equity for all employees, not just managers, is SRC. For this reason, it is further along the path toward entrepreneurialism than either Pepsi or Hyatt. Good management starts at the top, and SRC is no exception. Jack Stack, CEO of SRC, epitomizes the dynamic leader who leads and still is able to listen. He has the utmost respect for the ability and intelligence of his employees and treats them as equals.

In recent meetings, Stack spent several days talking to small groups of machinists, janitors, and white-collar employees about the company and what he feels is a need for a new entrepreneurial spirit. He talked about changes that are needed. This discussion occurred despite SRC's profits and its well-publicized success. Such discussions are what makes SRC unique. It is constantly innovating. One wanting a photograph of its success must settle for a moving picture.

Stack talks to employees about what he sees as everyone's need for career paths and opportunities to achieve. On the other hand, he feels management often ends up saying no to those who want more. If everyone stays in the same spot and at the same pay grade, where do you go?

Stack believes the answer to this problem and the problem of empowerment is for companies to get into the process of building businesses within their business. Empowerment comes by giving people the authority to run their own business. For instance, if you provide a general foreman with the opportunity to run his or her own business with SRC as parent corporation, this step has a cascade effect; it opens up other positions, for as one person starts his or her own business, others must be brought in to take the place of the one who left.

Stack says when SRC employees start a new business, SRC will look internally to see who is ready to replace those people. He believes SRC's mission, in the next ten years, is to create ten companies within the original company, all of which will be run by former SRC employees.

Stack plans to put people in those SRC spin-off companies who he feels can succeed. So that they will be prepared to run their own business, they will be taught about financing it and about cash flow. He points out that the process of preparing people to run their own company even helps SRC's management because to teach them, management must understand finance better and what it takes to make a company work.

WHY DO IT?

Stack told employees, "You can get into your own company with very little capital and make a lot of money if you are willing to learn." He emphasized that if they doubted his words, they need only look at SRC's parent corporation. The management at SRC got into this $40 million business with $100,000 in cash (20 percent of this deal was put up by Stack himself). He borrowed $10,000 and another $10,000 was loaned to him by his father-in-law. He said that he and his management team created SRC from almost nothing and that they would like to make the company more profitable by supporting people who take risks and putting them into business for themselves. The rationale is for SRC to keep regenerating itself.

Stack believes SRC's management knows how to create this opportunity for entrepreneurialism. The real question is whether SRC has the people who want to take advantage of the opportunity. The first step is to want it. Second, he stresses, come in and say you want to do it. Then SRC's management will help you assess what you think you need to do to get stronger in any particular area. Stack says SRC will bring in the people to teach you how to correct those weaknesses. What the company is looking for and the question he wants each employee to ask is, "Do I have the leadership to be able to take a company and run it?" In closing out his meeting he narrowed his eyes on the group and said, "The bottom line is that we believe in employee participation and think smallness is better than big and that we are scared about how big we are becoming."

QUESTION AND ANSWER

As the meeting ended, Stack faced the familiar question about what type of business SRC was considering establishing. He responded, "I would consider anything, but first you would have to put the financial to it." He stressed that if your business proposal involved using SRC's equipment or strict reliance on SRC's parent corporation (except for sales), he would say no.

On the other hand, if an employee wanted to rebuild turbo chargers (SRC rebuilds diesel and gasoline engines) and wanted to rent space to get into the charger business, SRC would definitely consider the proposal. Of course, he said, it would want to make sure you had the talent and training to succeed. However, if someone were simply going to cart out things, then all you would be doing is creating more paperwork and more nightmares.

SRC wants former employees to go into a business with a product line and grow that line into other products. SRC does not want people simply to leave the parent corporation or to be totally reliant on SRC for their business. Furthermore, Stack says the move has to make sense for both those leaving and those staying. It has to be a win/win situation.

Another employee asked Stack, "How much growth are you looking at in these start-up businesses?" The answer Stack gave was that SRC was not looking for a certain amount of growth each year. What it really wanted was that new start-ups would not run out of cash and not destroy SRC from within. The first priority was security.

Finally, one employee asked, "Do start-ups have to have anything to do with what SRC now does?" The answer was no. Stack did point out that if someone wanted to set up a barber shop, it had to compete with other opportunities. For instance, he had been contacted by one company that wanted SRC to package a "kit" that consisted of various automotive parts sold to this company's customers. Stack said: "That's an opportunity! I know because we costed it, cash flowed it, submitted it for quotation." If the idea goes, SRC's job is to find someone who understands this business, cash flow, scheduling, and turning inventories. He said that this business alone was an $8 million opportunity. The point is that when SRC has that kind of deal, it is difficult to look at a liquor store. However, Stack reemphasized that there are no boundaries to what it would consider.

SPIN-OFFS

Each of SRC's spin-off ventures started inside the company. The heads of these ventures are employees fully vested in SRC's ESOP. They cashed in their ESOP holdings to get the money to start their ventures. They literally bought themselves a new job, and they started these ventures with no safety net from SRC. They take the same risks borne by anyone starting a new business. SRC does not guarantee them their old jobs if their ventures fail.

Does it take a special type of person to launch ventures like these? Much entrepreneurship literature gives us lists of personal traits that supposedly improve one's chances of success in starting a new venture, as if only certain personality types are likely to succeed as entrepreneurs. In practice we can find many personality types among successful new ventures. SRC's experience bears out this point.

Jim Avery started a plant in Willow Springs, a small town about 80 miles from Springfield. This plant, Avatar, remanufactured those Oldsmobile diesel engines mentioned earlier. He set up and ran production in that plant. Bev Willis went with him to set up the plant's administrative services. Both got a taste of starting and running a separate operation.

Avery never got it out of his system. He submitted several financial plans after returning from the Willow Springs plant. He asked if he might take water pumps out of the business and start his own product line. One day a customer asked SRC to build torque amplifiers. SRC managers thought about Avery's previous request and wondered if he could produce this product. They reasoned that their plant had too little capacity for torque amplifiers. They also knew these amplifiers could yield them only a small profit margin. Considering these facts, they gave Avery the product. Within six months, he got a building in a nearby small town and developed the product from ground zero. He is selling $50,000–$87,000 per month and has yet to have a warranty claim.

When Avatar began to grow, Avery needed help supervising his workers, and hired an experienced lead man from SRC. By not replacing this man, SRC took $25,000 of overhead expense out of its core business. As Avatar continued to grow, Avery found his growing inventory becoming hard to manage. He went back to SRC and hired an inventory manager. SRC didn't replace him. Result: Another $25,000 in overhead saved.

Willis also wanted to start her own business. She holds an M.B.A. degree, specializing in accounting, but she knew nothing about sales. SRC put her in charge of the Customer Services Department for two years. Along came the opportunity to make and sell engine rebuilding kits, requiring no technical knowledge about engines, simply taking items from a shelf and packing them in a box. A person who would manage this business should have good sales, accounting, and inventory management skills. Perfect for Willis. She started and runs Newstream Enterprises profitably. Later, she hired one of SRC's engineers who specializes in packaging. The result is that SRC took two people out of its firm and spun off a $6 million per year business. Since it didn't replace these two, it cut $60,000 of overhead in its core business. The rest of Newstream's employees are temporaries paid $6 per hour.

SRC owns 51 percent of Newstream. Engines Plus is the only venture with managers who own an equity share. Eric Paulson owns 25 percent, and SRC owns 75 percent. The arrangement was 80/20 until six months ago when Paulson got an idea about how to manage his fast-growing business better.

Paulson did $300,000 of business the first year and $750,000 the second, and he expects to do $3.5 million during his third year. He operates two locations. One rebuilds oil coolers and exchanges rebuilt engines, while the other builds stationary power units. Paulson found two brothers to help him run each of his two locations. He asked SRC if he could buy another 5 percent of the business and sell it to his two managers. Now each of them owns 2.5 percent of the business. All SRC's new venture managers are seeking equity positions in the businesses they run. For example, Avery wants to own 20 percent of Avatar. SRC will negotiate a 100 percent equity sale with any venture whose entrepreneur is ready to buy. It will base the price on some multiple of the venture's earnings, as is typical in business sales.

CONCLUDING THOUGHTS

In closing one of his numerous meetings with his employees, Stack reflected on what is happening in corporate America, whether publishing books, making cars, or whatever: "We have all these really smart people. They all went through the right training programs and obtained a position of responsibility. They got to know their job better than anyone else and then—in the worst of all sins—are not allowed to participate in terms of equity."

He feels we are likely to see a real demise of corporate America if things continue the way they are. In many older corporations, there are two people on retirement for each one working. Costs are running rampant. Companies with that kind of overhead are not going to be able to compete with a start-up company like SRC because of its small liability.

For those companies with more retired employees than working employees, he says you are going to see them trying to reduce overhead, trying to operate with fewer and fewer people. Companies that have 100,000 employees can incur millions of dollars in health care costs alone. Most companies do not make this kind of money. Competing against start-up companies with no such overhead is even more critical. SRC is preparing for the future by parting out its business. That is why Stack says it is continually going to make start-ups and create new companies. The advantage is flexibility and speed. Additionally, if it is good at it, in 30 years or so, it will not face the overhead and crisis many companies are already facing.

REFERENCES

Ellis, James E. "Feeling Stuck at Hyatt? Create a New Business." *Business Week*, December 10, 1990, 195.
"PepsiCo SharePower We All Have a Stake." *PepsiCo, Inc.* 20, no. 4 (August-September 1989): 2.
Solomon, Tolie. "Pepsi Offers Stock Options to All, Not Just Honchos." *Wall Street Journal*, June 28, 1989, pp. B1,3.

Bibliography

Aguilar, Francis J. "CRAY Research: Preparing for the 1990s." *Harvard Business School Case Studies*, January 17, 1990, 8.

Alinsworth, Susan. "160 Heads Are Better Than 7." (Hoechst Celanese in-house publication) *Reporter* 3, no. 3 (Fall 1989): 16–17.

Alster, Norm. "What Flexible Workers Can Do." *Fortune*, February 13, 1990, 66.

Banas, Paul A. *The Relationship Between Participative Management and Employee Involvement at Ford Motor Company* (in-house publication), May 16, 1984, 1–2.

————. "Employee Involvement: A Sustained Labor/Management Initiative at the Ford Motor Company." In John P. Campbell and Richard J. Campbell, *Productivity in Organizations New Perspectives from Industrial and Organizational Psychology*. San Francisco: Jossey-Bass, 1988.

Baumann, M. "Cart Titled Family Business." *News-Leader*, November 26, 1990, D1.

Benke, Ralph Jr., and Robert H. Hermanson. "Be a Better Teacher." *Management Accounting* 71 (April 1990): 561.

Braun, Kay Bender. "A Tale of Two Teams." (Hoechst Celanese in-house publication) *Reporter* 5, no. 1 (Spring 1990): 18–19.

Bryne, John. "Is Research in the Ivory Tower Fuzzy, Irrelevant, Pretentious." *Business Week*, October 29, 1990, 62.

Bunke, Harvey C. "Pax Americana." *Business Horizons*, January-February 1990.

Carnevale, Anthony P., and Leila J. Gainer. *The Learning Enterprise*. U.S. Department of Labor Employment and Training Administration. February 1989, 3.

Clurman, Carol. "More Than Just a Paycheck." *USA Weekend*, January 19–21, 1990.

Denison, E. F. *Trends in American Economic Growth 1929–1982*. Washington, DC: Brookings Institution, 1985.

Denton, D. Keith. "Better Management Through Budgeting: Instilling a Quality Culture." *Management Review*, October 1988, 16–18.

Deutschman, Alan. "Pioneers of the New Balance." *Fortune*, May 20, 1991, 60–68.

Dreyfuss, Joel. "The Three R's on the Shop Floor." *Fortune* (Special Issue), Spring 1990, 91–92.

Drucker, Peter F. "Workers' Hands Bound by Tradition." *Wall Street Journal*, August 2, 1988, 2.

Dryfuss, Joe. "Get Ready for the New Work Force." *Fortune*, April 23, 1990, 165–68.

Dumaine, Brian. "How Managers Can Succeed Through Speed." *Fortune*, February 13, 1989, 57.

———. "Making Education Work." *Fortune* (Special Issue), Spring 1990, 12.

———. "Who Needs a Boss?" *Fortune*, May 7, 1990, 58.

Dwyer, Carol A. "Teamwork Pays Off." *Monogram* (General Electric in-house publication) 68, no. 2 (Spring 1990): 12–17.

Elfin, Mel. "Getting Back to Basics." *U.S. News and World Report*, October 15, 1990, 104.

Ellis, James E. "Feeling Stuck at Hyatt? Create a New Business." *Business Week*, December 10, 1990, 195.

Faltermayer, Edmund. "Is 'Made in U.S.A.' Fading Away?" *Fortune*, September 24, 1990, 62–64.

Farnham, Alan. "The Trust Gap." *Fortune*, December 4, 1989, 70.

Fein, Mitchell. *IMPROSHARE: An Alternative to Traditional Managing*. Norcross, GA: Mitchell Fein, Inc. Institute of Industrial Engineering, 1991, 43.

Fierman, Jaclyn. "Shaking the Blue-Collar Blues." *Fortune*, April 22, 1991, 216–17.

"The Flap over Executive Pay." *Business Week*, May 6, 1991, 90–93.

Flextime Implementation Guidelines (Merck's in-house publication), Human Resources Planning and Development, February 1981.

Ford Education and Personnel Research Development. *Continuous Improvement Through Participation* (booklet), September 1984, 6.

Green, Dick. "The Real Facts About 'BASHING,' Justification, and CIM or cIM." *Industrial Engineering* 22, no. 6 (1990): 4.

Henkoff, Ronald. "Cost Cutting: How to Do It Right." *Fortune*, April 9, 1990, 40–48.

———. "Make Your Office More Productive." *Fortune*, February 25, 1991, 76.

Hewlett, William R. "The Human Side of Management." *Eugene B. Clark Executive Lecture*. University of Notre Dame, March 25, 1982, 9.

Jacob, Nancy L., James E. Reinmuth, and Robert S. Hamada. *Final Report on the AACSB Task Force on Research*, January 1987, 4. AACSB, St. Louis, Missouri.

Kraar, Louis. "Japan's Gung-Ho U.S. Car Plants." *Fortune*, January 30, 1989, 104.

———. "25 Who Help the U.S. Win." *Fortune* (Special Issue), 1991, 39–45.

Main, Jeremy. "The Winning Organization." *Fortune*, September 26, 1988, 56.

———. "Computers of the World Unite!" *Fortune*, September 24, 1990, 115.

A Manager's Guide to Face-to-Face Communication Meetings (booklet published by Merck & Co.)

Maraniss, David. "Firm Makes Radical Revolution from Top Down." *Washington Post*, March 8, 1990, 1.

"Marriott Corporation: High School Awareness Program." *Inside Marriott* (Marriott news and information report).

Metropolitan Life Insurance Company. *The National Work Team Leaders' Guide to the Quality Improvement Process.* 1986, 37.

"More Than a Gut Feeling." *Exchange* (Hewlett-Packard in-house publication), December–January 1988, 14.

O'Connell, Frances. "Who's on Second? Everyone!" (Hoechst Celanese in-house publication) *Reporter* 4, no. 1 (Winter 1990): 8–9.

"P and Q Survey." *Focus. Industrial Engineering* 1990, 6.

"Pepsico SharePower We All Have a Stake." *PepsiCo. Inc.* 20, no. 4 (August–September 1989): 2.

Perry, Nancy J. "Here Come Richer, Riskier Pay Plans." *Fortune*, December 19, 1988, 51–58.

―――. "The Workers of the Future." *Fortune* (Special Issue), 1991, 68–72.

Peters, Tom. "Competitiveness Requires Trust, Appreciation of Workers." *Springfield News Leader*, August 27, 1990, D–1.

Porter, Lyman W., and Lawrence E. McKibbin. "Management Education and Development: Drift or Thrust into the 21st Century." *Executive Summary.* AACSB, St. Louis, Missouri.

Quickel, Stephen W. "Welch on Welch." *Financial World* 159, no. 7 (April 3, 1990): 3.

Rasmussen, MaryAnne E. "American Express: Quality Culture Our Key to Motivating Employees." *American Productivity and Quality Center Executive Center*, August 4, 1988.

Rice, Faye. "Champions of Communications." *Fortune*, June 3, 1991, 111–20.

Richman, Louis S. "The Coming World Labor Shortage." *Fortune*, April 9, 1990, 76.

Rodgers, T. J. "No Excuses Management." *Harvard Business Review*, July–August, 1990, 85.

Savoie, Ernest J. *Creating the Work Force of the Future: The Ford Focus* (in-house publication), September 16, 1986, 6.

"The Secret of Our Success." *Exchange* (Hewlett-Packard in-house publication), October–November 1987, 11.

Sellers, Patricia. "Pepsi Keeps on Going After No. 1." *Fortune*, March 11, 1991, 63.

Sheridan, John H. "Lean but Not Mean." *Business Week*, February 19, 1990, 53.

Sherman, Stratford. "Inside the Mind of Jack Welch." *Fortune*, March 27, 1989, 38.

"The Skill of Recruiting." *Employee Relations: The Challenge Ahead* (Merck in-house publication).

Smith, Bill. *The Motorola Story* (in-house publication).

Solomon, Tolie. "Pepsi Offers Stock Options to All, Not Just Honchos." *Wall Street Journal*, June 28, 1989.

Stephens, Sam. "Yes, I Can Make a Difference in the Labor Crisis." *Acclaim*, 11.

Stewart, Thomas A. "So You Push Your People Too Hard?" *Fortune*, October 22, 1990, 124.

———. "The New American Century Where We Stand." *Fortune* (Special Issue), 1991, 14–22.

Stine, Andrea. "Design for Decision Making." (Hoechst Celanese in-house publication) *Reporter* 3, no. 2 (July 1989): 7–10.

"Teamwork—More Critical Today Than Ever Before." *Quality Performance* 7, no. 9 (May 31, 1990): 2.

"Three Teachers Hit the Labs." *Reporter* (Hoechst Celanese in-house publication) 2, no. 3 (December 1988): 6.

Tichy, Noel, and Ram Charan. "Speed, Simplicity, Self-Confidence." *Harvard Business Review*, September–October 1989, 115.

Toch, Thomas. "A Return to Teaching." *U.S. News and World Report*, October 15, 1990, 107.

Trunick, Perry A. "Leadership and People Distinguish Federal Express." *Transportation and Distribution*, December 1989, 19.

Ulrich, Dave, and Dale Lake. "Organizational Capability: Creating Competitive Advantage." *Academy of Management Executive* 5, no. 1 (February 1991): 80.

Voss, Charles E. "Applied Techniques for Higher Employee Involvement." *1991 Manufacturing Principles and Practices Seminar*. Orlando, FL, April 22–24, 1991, 177.

Wagel, William H. "Working (and Managing) Without Supervisors." *Personnel*, September 1987, 8–11.

Watson, Thomas J. *A Business and Its Beliefs*. New York: McGraw-Hill, 1963, 13.

Webber, Alan M. "Consensus, Continuity, and Common Sense." *Harvard Business Review* 68 (July–August 1990): 116.

Weber, Joseph. "No Bosses and Even 'Leaders' Can't Give Orders." *Business Week*, December 10, 1990, 196–97.

Weber, Joseph, Lisa Driscoll, and Richard Brandt. "Farewell, Fast Track." *Business Week*, December 10, 1990, 192–96.

Wiggenhorn, Bill. "Achieving Six Sigma Quality." *Opportunities* 5, no. 2 (February 1988): 2.

Index

About the Author

D. KEITH DENTON is Professor of Management at Southwest Missouri State University. He has published eight other practitioner oriented books and his articles have appeared in over 70 national management magazines and journals.